COLERAINE

AND THE CAUSEWAY COAST

NICOLA PIERCE is a freelance writer, who has co-written *The Last Executioner*, *Angel of Bang Kwang* and *Ms Bangkok*, all of which are published by Maverick House. She is also the author of *Ballymena: City of the Seven Towers* and *Lisburn: Phoenix from the Flames*, which are published by The Brehon Press. Nicola currently lives in Belfast.

STEPHEN STEWART is a Ballymena-based freelance photographer, who specialises in landscape and architectural photography in Northern Ireland. He has previously contributed photographs to the book *Ballymena: City of the Seven Towers*. Further examples of his work can be found at stephenstewartphotography.co.uk.

COLERAINE

AND THE CAUSEWAY COAST

Nicola Pierce (signature)

Nicola Pierce

Photography by
Stephen Stewart

W
Waterstone's

Published for Waterstone's Booksellers Ltd in 2008
by The Brehon Press Ltd
1A Bryson Street
Belfast BT5 4ES
Northern Ireland

Text © 2008 Nicola Pierce
Photography © 2008 Stephen Stewart

ISBN: 978 1 905474 30 1

Cover design and picture layout by Jake Campbell
Printed and bound by J H Haynes & Co Ltd, Sparkford

CONTENTS

Acknowledgements 7

PART ONE: ORIGINS 11

PART TWO: FAMOUS CONNECTIONS 43

PART THREE: AROUND COLERAINE 107

Useful Websites 117

Bibliography 118

Index 121

LIMITED EDITION

This book is number ___606___

of ___1000___ copies printed

ACKNOWLEDGMENTS

The author wishes to thank the following for their help in making this book possible:

Helen Campbell and Paula Fleming, of Waterstone's in Coleraine, for their support and encouragement;

Pat Ramsey for the hours it took to lay out the text;

Jake Campbell for designing the wonderful cover and picture sections;

My colleagues at Waterstone's in Ballymena for their friendship and support: Damian, Roger, Victoria, Jonathan, Ian, Carrie, Louise, Jennifer and Pamela;

And last, but by no means least, Stephen Stewart, a wonderful photographer and a genuine artist!

for Lynn and Rachel

PART ONE
ORIGINS

The Name

Coleraine (Cúil Rathin), which translates as 'corner/nook of ferns', or 'ferny corner', was the original name of the county of Londonderry. It is thought that Saint Patrick was responsible for the name; when he visited the area in 450AD the local chieftain gave him a bit of land on which to build a church and because it was covered with ferns Patrick named it 'Cúil Rathain'. That first church which Patrick built is quite possibly the site of the magnificent St Patrick's that stands today just off the Diamond. The Honourable Irish Society found it necessary, in 1614, to improve and strengthen the church which had the unenviable habit of being regularly plundered by marauding invaders.

The Town

Coleraine is a large town situated on the River Bann, fifty-five miles northwest of Belfast and thirty miles east of Derry City, with a population of approximately 24,000, whose disposable income is well above the Northern Ireland average, as are the house prices.

There is evidence of Anglo-Norman settlement, from the twelfth to the fourteenth centuries, in the surrounding area of Coleraine while the town itself dates from the plantation of Derry. The central square, 'The Diamond' dates from 1611, which is when the Honourable Irish Society established a port on the site.

In the 1500s the area of Coleraine was 'owned' by the O'Cahans, friends and staunch supporters of the O'Neill clan, ready to take up arms on their behalf against foreign enemies. The chief of this clan, Hugh O'Neill (1550-1616), was also known as the Baron of Dungannon and then later the Earl of Tyrone; in other words, he had a love/hate relationship with the English Crown: while accepting their titles he wished for an end to English rule in Ireland. Undoubtedly his friendship with the O'Cahans tottered when one of the younger generation told tales on O'Neill, going straight to the Bishop of Derry as well as to the council in Dublin Castle, no less, to inform them about Hugh's big plan to overthrow the English in Ulster. Naturally a whole lot of trouble followed which resulted, in 1607, in the infamous Flight of the Earls. The Irish chieftains were obliged, in order to evade capture—or worse—by the English, to leave their estates and homes for the shores of France and Italy. Hugh brought his family to Rome and it is said that right up until his dying day, in 1616, he was still full of remorse for making that difficult decision to leave his country behind forever.

Meanwhile King James I, through his Lord Deputy, Sir Arthur Chichester (1563-1625), collected up, or confiscated, approximately 500,000 acres of land throughout Tyrone, Donegal, Coleraine, Fermanagh, Armagh and Cavan that was previously the domain of the emigrated Ulster clans. He had his own plan for the area, to reform it with law, religion and brand new inhabitants in the shape of English and Scot settlers, therefore bringing it in line with the rest of his kingdom, ridding himself of the troublesome, and up to now, persistent worry of rebellion.

The Honourable Irish Society/Plantation of Coleraine

This organisation was set up in 1609 to supervise the plantation of Derry, with the hope that it would be central to the plantation of the whole of Ulster. Because there was no state money to fund the work the authorities looked to private capital. It was surveyor, and merchant venturer, Sir Thomas Phillips' idea that merchants should plant the county of Coleraine. Phillips had received a grant of land from the King, which included leasing the town of Toome but he felt vulnerable to attack from resentful Irish natives, those followers of O'Neill and O'Cahan who continued to lurk about in the shadows of the woods. Naturally he would feel a lot more settled and secure if he was surrounded by a large number of neighbours of his own kind. In order to sell the plantation of Coleraine as a plausible venture Sir Thomas needed to make it as attractive a prospective as possible. He suggested that the future town could be perfect for the business of grinding oats, making linen, establishing breweries and tanning houses, as well as ship-building; not to mention the extensive forests and rivers full of salmon. In other words, Coleraine as a potential money-making investment, was in all likelihood a very safe bet.

Accordingly twelve of London's most successful companies were approached and invited to take part in the project. A special meeting of aldermen was called on 1 July 1609. The companies were varied in their specialties: Goldsmiths, Grocers, Fishmongers, Haberdashers, Clothworkers, Merchant Tailors, Ironmongers, Mercers, Vintners, Salters, Drapers and Skinners. They weren't immediately enthused; for instance, the Fishmongers wondered aloud whether it would be best to stay out of this type of thing as it was bound to be very expensive. In fact they had to be coerced, especially the smaller businesses who fretted that the vast enterprise would break them. Besides, who in their right mind would want to leave the splendid city of London and move to the 'badlands' of Ulster?

Up to that point Coleraine would have been pretty much a wilderness of forest and lowlands inhabited by the uncouth, and probably dangerous (as far as the English were concerned), native population. Naturally King James I was delighted to be told his dream for Ulster was about to be fulfilled, that the land would soon be planted with English settlers, and he gave his blessing to the Society, excited for the task to be completed as soon as possible. No pressure then!

The decision regarding the town of Coleraine was thus: it was to be built on the Abbey side of the Bann. One hundred houses were to be erected with room being made available for two hundred more. All construction of houses and fortifications in Coleraine and Derry were to be finished by 1 November 1611.

No doubt the businessmen embarked on their collaborative project with a sense of duty and importance; however, it would not be an easy road. Work began on Coleraine in a spurt of excitement before slowly grinding to a halt. Three men were entrusted with travelling to the area and supervising the 130 workers and, unfortunately for all involved, these men, Tristram Beresford, John Rowley and William Gage, were more interested in fleecing the forests of wood in order to sell it for their own gains as opposed to motivating the carpenters, builders and masons, who, having been paid three months in advance, became bored and resentful. The Crown was most displeased with both the slow progress of the operation and the Society for failing to carry out one of the major stipulations. They were supposed to remove the native Irish from the land and this they failed to do, having decided that they needed the locals to provide food for the settlements, or else work as labourers. Furthermore, any Gaelic Irish with money could potentially be tenants, paying rents to their English landlords, so it made sense to keep them around. Meanwhile, as far as the Crown was concerned, this was the whole point of the plantation, i.e. getting rid of the pesky natives and substituting them with God/King-fearing citizens. And the natives were a bother. At one point it was reported that English workers would not venture into the woods unless they were accompanied by—at least—eleven other colleagues, owing to the number of attacks being made on the new settlers. There was also the panic-inducing rumour that Hugh O'Neill was on his way back at any minute to reclaim his land with the help of a massive army.

A highly irritated James sent over Nicholas Pynnar to make out a thorough report on the progress of the plantation—and the news about Coleraine was not good. Pynnar described a filthy, dirty, ramshackle town with only three houses and too few inhabitants to defend it should it come under attack.

In 1635 the twelve businesses were fined a serious £70,000 by the Crown for their failure to correctly perform what they had signed up to do; furthermore, the Charter of the Irish Society was shelved. It would be a long time before the Charter was renewed; another twenty-seven years before the Society could begin their work again, which included building the walled city of Derry.

Despite the problems of corrupt officials and workers turning into alcoholics, for the want of something better to do, the building of Coleraine was completed by 1612. English settlers had began to arrive in 1611 to pay rent on some 116 houses which were built on the streets that are still there today: Bridge Street, Abbey Street, Church Street and New Row.

Market House

In 1742 it was decided that Coleraine needed a centre point in the town, perhaps a market house. Thanks to the Irish Society, which made a provision of £700 (some say £900) along with thirty-five tons of timber, work began on just such a building. The man responsible for the design was George Dance, the Elder (1695-1768), a London architect who had a wealth of experience constructing public buildings like the neo-Palladian Mansion House (1739-1752), and churches like St Botolph-without-Bishopsgate (1725) and St Matthew's, Bethnal Green (1743-1746).

At the time of his contract in Coleraine he was the City of London surveyor, thus one of the top men in his field, and the Market House seems to be the only building he designed outside of England, a privilege indeed.

The project was completed the following year, comprised of a two storey building which provided an official location for important meetings and legal proceedings in its first floor court house while the ground floor was strictly commercial in purpose, with arcades or arches serving as individual shop stalls from where a variety of produce was sold. In 1830 a clock was inserted in the tower thanks to the Marquis of Waterford.

(The infamous Marquis of Waterford may or may not have been 'Spring-Heeled Jack', a mad man who preyed particularly on young women in London throughout the 1830s. Eyewitnesses reported him wearing a long black cloak, plus he had a freakish ability to jump over walls that were much too high for any normal person. Dozens of people claimed to have seen him jumping from rooftop to rooftop and to have heard his loud, manic laugh. The Marquis, a rich, young Irish nobleman, was suspected thanks to his taste for cruel, bad jokes and overall negative attitude to women. He was also allegedly in the area when many of the attacks took place, and the most damning evidence is that of a servant boy who rushed to help a young girl in his clutches, and who swore that he saw the letter 'W' on the attacker's black cloak. The fantastic jumping ability was thought to be a result of mechanics, springs in the shoes and—apparently—the Marquis hung out with friends who had studied applied mechanics. However, the police changed their minds about the Marquis after the Irish man was fatally thrown from his horse in 1859 and the attacks continued. The last recorded sighting of Jack took place in Liverpool in 1904, although there could have been more than one Spring-Heeled Jack, which is what some people believe today.)

The Town Hall

Just over a hundred years later, in 1855, a group of builders examined the Market House and made a worrying discovery: parts of the wooden roof were rotting away while cracks had appeared in the corner of the south-east wall. It was decided to knock it down and replace it with a new building, a proper Town Hall. There were initial debates about moving the location of this important building to the west end of Bridge Street; however, the traditional location won out and the Town Hall was built on the exact spot of the Market House. Once again the Irish Society came through, with a grant of £2,000. The new hall was designed by architect Thomas Turner and built by McLaughlin & Harvey to the tune of £4,416.19s.10d, one thousand pounds more than the initial estimate. The material used was golden sandstone which gives the building a sort of sun-dried Italian country villa look. McLaughlin & Harvey, a Belfast firm, was founded in 1853 and is one of the biggest contractors in Northern Ireland today. Numerous functions were performed at the new premises; sometimes it was a library, or a newsroom, and at other times it was a Ballast Office or a Savings Bank when it was not holding a Mayor's Court or Quarter Sessions. Whatever was going on between the walls of the building it was always the focal point of the busy town.

In 1914 a stained glass window, commemorating the tercentenary (300th anniversary) of The Honourable Irish Society, made by the Campbell brothers of Belfast, was inserted. It depicts four elements of the town's history: the restored Parish Church of 1775, the Diamond in 1815, the Salmon Leap in 1836, and the Irish Society Schools in 1869. The Campbell brothers were also involved in the three major stained glass windows on Belfast's City Hall (Queen Victoria, Saint George, Belfast City Seal) as well as the windows of Derry's Guildhall.

But, of course, Coleraine is a lot, lot older than the buildings that were erected in 1610. Long before the English settlers arrived Coleraine was playing host to all manner of residents.

Mount Sandel

The Mesolithic period stretched from 7,000 to 4,000BC, and was the beginning of it all—that is, today's highly populated island. The emerging Stone Age waved goodbye to the retreating Ice Age and—thanks to the mammoth discovery that stones weren't just for throwing but could also be transformed into tools—welcomed the tentative beginnings of a brand new trend: farming.

While we cannot be sure how they got here, we do know that, in approximately 7,000BC, there were people here; hunting, eating, making tools to hunt for food, eating, taking their pick of trees to fell from the massive forests that used to cover the terrain in order to cook food, eating, storing food, eating, building shelters, and, well, eating. And we know this much thanks largely to Mount Sandel fort, which is reputed to be the oldest settled site in the land. While the weather was probably not too different from today for those early dwellers, they did have a lot more variety in terms of flora and fauna. In fact a lot of what was available at that time could be found in Europe. Humans shared the forests with large mammals, such as wild pigs and bears, while the rivers were pregnant with salmon and eels.

As the Mesolithic period progressed there was good news and bad news in relation to the climate, it got warmer but wetter. Fortunately our ancestors had the good sense to erect roofs over themselves, from which they could moodily stare out at yet another rainy day. An archaeological dig in the early 1970s revealed a series of stake holes in the ground, which confirmed that Mount Sandel would have contained circular huts with a width of approximately twenty feet. There also appeared to be storage pits in and around the huts, presumably to hoard and protect their inhabitants' provisions from other carnivores. Their diet was rich in protein; the dig unearthed the burnt bones of birds, pigs, hares, salmon, trout and eels, as well as hazelnut shells, and apple and water lily seeds.

Coleraine and the World Wars

The contribution which the brave young men of Coleraine and its surrounding area made as combatants in the First World War is marked by the statue of the noble soldier that is the War Memorial, which stands to the east of the Town Hall. It was built in 1922 after the locals raised a massive £1,800 to commemorate their dead. The names of those heroes who fought the good fight in the Second World War are also represented.

Of course the First World War was not the first time that local men signed up to fight for their country. Quite a few had taken part in conflicts like the Boer and Crimean Wars, some making a name for themselves in the process. One such man was Marshall Sir George Stuart White (1835-1912) from Portstewart, who was awarded that most prestigious of British military honours, the Victoria Cross, for outstanding bravery in the 1879 Battle of Chrasia in India during the Afghan War (1878-1880).

It was 6 October 1879 and the 92nd Regiment of the Gordon Highlanders had been trying to force the enemy from their stronghold position on a steep hill. Unfortunately all the effort and spent artillery proved to be in vain. Major (which is what he was at the time) White decided that there was no alternative but to have his men climb the hill and force the enemy into close combat. He led the way with two companies of his regiment in his wake. The climb was difficult, especially following a tough battle, and the men were exhausted by the time the enemy was sighted. There was neither the time nor the freedom to take a break, as their only hope lay in a surprise attack; meanwhile, the number of enemy combatants was a lot more than previously thought—the Major reckoned his men were outnumbered by approximately eight to one. It must have been a quick decision—maybe a completely impulsive one—but the Major, on realising the madness, not to mention probable danger, of asking his tired soldiers to immediately confront a bigger army, took a rifle and continued on by himself. One might wonder whether he had to sternly order his men to wait where they were—surely some of them insisted on accompanying him—or perhaps he told them to catch their breath and snuck off without warning. However it came about, he got so close to the enemy that he was able to choose his target and fire, shooting dead the other group's leader. This caused panic in the opposition's ranks which triggered a voluntary evacuation, and the fortified position was won.

He proved himself again a year later, on 1 September 1880, at the Battle of Kandahar, when he led a final charge in the face of heavy bombardment, thanks to two big guns. The Major, once more, went in for an immediate confrontation with the enemy. Having ridden up close enough to spot the guns, and without stopping to think, he threw himself at the nearest one and seized it, causing the enemy to flee. His Victoria Cross is on display at the Gordon Highlanders Museum in Aberdeen, Scotland.

The repercussions of the Battle of the Somme reverberated throughout the houses of Coleraine and the surrounding areas. Nearly every street was in mourning for a young man who had made the decision to leave behind everything he knew—family, job, neighbours, home—and volunteer to take up the fight against Germany in a strange land he had probably never heard of before. There was a tremendous loss of life suffered by the British army on 1 July 1916. Twenty thousand men died on one terrible day while the number of casualties ran to approximately fifty-eight thousand.

Second Lieutenant Robert Wallace Gilmour, of the 9th Royal Inniskilling Fusiliers, is listed on the Pozieres Memorial to the

Missing, which means he has no known grave. He was from the Diamond in Coleraine and had been working in Dublin for the Ulster Bank. Second Lieutenant William James Knox Bell, of the 9th Siege Battery Royal Garrison Artillery is buried at the Bertrancourt Military Cemetery. The twenty-eight-year-old, the only son of James and Fanny Jane, was from Ashbrook in Coleraine. Another local, Private Arnold Wilkinson, from the 6th Black Watch, is buried in the Mailly Wood Cemetery, near Amiens. Private Edward Reid Dallas, from Church Street, Coleraine, lies buried in the Ancre British Cemetery. There are many, many more.

Another local man was awarded the Victoria Cross for his bravery in battle. Private Robert Quigg, 12th Battalion Royal Irish Rifles (Ulster Division), hailed from Carnkirk, in Bushmills. He was born in 1885, the son of Mr Robert Quigg who was in the enviable position of being paid to work as a guide at the splendid Giant's Causeway. The younger Robert worked on the Bushmills estate of Sir Harry McNaghten, and was obviously very fond of his boss because when Sir Harry signed up to join the army so too did his thirty-one-year-old employee, who promised Sir Harry's father that he would do his very best to look after him.

On 1 July 1916 Private Quigg was with his platoon in Hamel in the north of France. It had been a tough day of constant fighting; the platoon had launched an assault three times against an entrenched enemy. You can imagine the terrific noise of screaming bullets with the constant threat of being hit, either dying outright or—much worse—being injured so badly as to be unable to make your way back to your own front line, along with the smell of blood and death, and the cries of the dying.

Early the following morning, on 2 July, a rumour spread throughout the platoon that their leader, Second Lieutenant Sir Edward Harry McNaghten, Bart., from Dundarave, Bushmills, had been hit but was possibly still alive, lying somewhere outside on No

Man's Land between the two armies. Private Robert Quigg went out to look for him, no mean feat in itself. It meant running across a stretch of land while having to constantly dodge enemy artillery, in the form of heavy shelling and machine gun fire, and search through scores of corpses for the wounded officer. Before he could locate Sir Harry he found another wounded soldier whom he picked up and brought back to relative safety. When he had delivered this man to the medics he went out for a second time and, once again, before he could locate McNaghten, he found another comrade who needed carrying back. Private Quigg went out a third time and was obliged to return with another wounded soldier. Bear in mind the amount of time it would have taken him to find a soldier and establish, under fire, how severe any injuries were, before lifting at least ten stone of dead weight to make his way, still avoiding gunfire, back to the British lines. In all Private Quigg went out seven times looking for his officer and each time he found someone else to rescue. The last man he grabbed was within a few yards of the enemy wire; he dragged this soldier across the field on a waterproof sheet. It was seven hours of unrelenting stress, both emotionally and physically, before the exhausted Quigg was forced to give up his search for Sir Harry. Some say that the private had to be physically restrained from going out again, but he had brought seven men home in Harry's place, a noble achievement.

(Two year later Hamel would be the location of a marvellous victory for a combination of Australian and American forces when, on 4 July 1918, they made an historic attack under General Monash, which involved for the first time infantry, artillery, tanks and parachute troops.)

It was discovered later that Sir Harry had been fatally injured just before the German trench and, when he fell, no less than three German officers had jumped out to take him prisoner, killing a brave soldier who had tried to prevent the Bushmills man from being captured. Sir Harry was the sixth Bart and the title, upon his death, should have passed to Second Lieutenant Sir Arthur Douglas McNaghten. However, before Sir Harry's death was officially confirmed, the nineteen-year-old Sir Arthur was also killed, on the Somme a few months later, on 15 September. He is buried there in the Caterpillar Valley Cemetery.

Meanwhile, Robert Quigg must have decided that the army life suited him. He stayed in the ranks for another eighteen years after that fateful day in Hamel, retiring as a sergeant in 1934. There is a wonderful tale that concerns his receiving the Victoria Cross from the King. Apparently, as His Highness solemnly handed Quigg his medal, he remarked that he was a very brave man, whereupon the humble Bushmills native, probably from nervousness and embarrassment, complimented the King in turn, saying, 'Ack, sure you're a brave wee man yourself!' When he died in 1955, Robert was buried at Billy Parish Churchyard, near Bushmills.

During the Second World War three American units were stationed at garrisons within the Coleraine Borough area. The 507th Parachute Infantry Regiment Troopers stayed at Landsdowne Crescent in Portrush, while Camp Cromore at Portstewart provided a temporary home to the 508th Parachute Infantry Regiment Troopers. This regiment had left New York during the night of 27-28 December 1944, on board the USAT *James Parker*. They arrived in Belfast Harbour on 9 January and travelled by train to Portstewart. Then, there was the 'E' Battery, the 80th Airborne Anti-Aircraft Artillery Battalion, which comprised a headquarter unit, a medical detachment, and six batteries of approximately eight men each, who spent some weeks training in Kilrea, under the command of Major Raymond Singleton, just before Christmas of 1943. They were preparing for the Normandy invasion, and would be involved in the liberation of the first French city, on 6 June.

Coleraine also had its own platoon, the 6th Light Anti-Aircraft Battery (Royal Artillery) Supplementary Reserve, also known as the 'Coleraine Battery'. It was made up of local volunteers at the beginning of the Second World War and their mission was to support the army against any attack from German forces. The Battery fought at major battles in Egypt and many others throughout Europe. When they returned to Coleraine at the end of the war they formed an Old Comrades' Association which met up every single year for the next half a century.

Thomas Knox Miller, from Coleraine, enlisted in the No 2 Londonderry County Battalion on 21 July 1940. Three years later he was promoted to sergeant. He was awarded the British Empire Medal (BEM) for his outstanding commitment, and for his performance at training exercises, which led him to being recognised as having the makings of the perfect instructor. The BEM was the Medal of the Order of the British Empire for Meritorious Service which recognised both civil and military service.

Coleraine's Local Newspapers

There were quite a few important events in 1844, the year before the Great Irish Famine. On 24 May, inventor Samuel Morse sent the first ever message over the first telegraph line from Washington to Baltimore, which read, 'What God hath wrought.' In June, Britain's new Factory Act declared that women could only work twelve hours a day whereas children, aged six to thirteen years, could not work more than six. The poet Gerard Manley Hopkins was born in July. England abolished jailing people for unpaid debts (years before America would do so) in August, while Queen Victoria opened the Royal Exchange two months later, in October, the same month that German philosopher Frederick Nietzsche was born. Nietzsche is widely quoted today for his views on religion, philosophy, and women; for example, 'Ah, women. They make the highs higher and the lows more frequent.' A Swedish chemistry professor, Gustaf Erik Pasch, invented the safety match, and the first ever international cricket match was played in New York City between Canada and the United States. The day of 22 October 1844 brought huge disappointment to the forerunners of the Seventh-day Adventist Church when Jesus Christ did not show up, as predicted by one William Miller, an American Baptist minister, following a close study of his Bible. Some of Miller's followers were so excited about the Son of God's second visit to earth that they neglected their farms and crops, and when there was a no show they were ruined, in more ways than one.

In November, Democrat James K Polk defeated Harry Clay, 170 votes to 105, to become the eleventh president of America. Polk was born in Mecklenburg County, North Carolina but his ancestors were among the first Ulster-Scots settlers to become a powerful political family, after emigrating to the US from Coleraine in 1680. He oversaw plenty of 'firsts' himself: America's first postage stamps, the opening of the US Naval Academy, and he was the first American president to be photographed frequently while he was in office. He was a popular president overall apart from one niggling area: slavery. A plantation and slave owner all his life, this only became a serious problem when he followed through on his expansionist policies, securing and buying up land to add to America, including the Oregon Territory (Washington, Oregon and Idaho) and Texas. His critics accused him of being a tool for slavery; as he expanded America's territory, so too was he making more widespread the practice of owning slaves.

1844 was a notable year for Coleraine, because this was the year in which it finally got its own newspaper, the *Coleraine Chronicle*, which was launched in April. This was also the year that the *Ulster Gazette* and *Tyrone Constitution* came into existence. Up to that point, perhaps, the locals read the *London-Derry Journal and*

General Advertiser, which had been around since June 1772 when it was just a four-page paper that came out twice a week and cost a penny. Initially the *Journal*'s writings would have had much in common with the Protestant community but then, in 1829, there was inevitable fallout after the paper voiced support for Catholic Emancipation. Its enraged editor, William Wallen, obviously did not share this view, which he swiftly demonstrated by leaving to set up the *Londonderry Sentinel and North West Advertiser* which was fortunate for him as the *Journal* only took on a more Nationalist leaning after his departure until eventually, in 1880, it changed its name to the *Derry Journal*.

The *Chronicle* began life in the office of the local printer, George V Robinson, who published it every Saturday, at 24 Lower Stone Road. When it first came out its name was frighteningly long: *The Coleraine Chronicle and Ballymena, Ballymoney, Bushmills, Dervock, Draperstown, Garragh, Kilrea, Maghera, Magherafelt, Moneymore, Newtownlimavady, Portstewart and Portrush Weekly Advisor* and, not surprisingly, it quickly underwent a name change to *The Coleraine Chronicle and North of Ireland Advisor*. The paper was liberal in its outlook and supported the likes of the tenant farmers, covering everything from marriages, deaths and the day-to-day life of the town. Later it moved to offices in Abbey Street. In or around 1851 local solicitor Hugh Boyd Mackay bought the paper from Robinson, and from 1852 to 1897 the *Chronicle* was edited by John McCombie, from Ross-shire, who was interested in land reform. McCombie died in 1904 at the grand old age of ninety years. His successor was John Shannon, whose four sons, John, Tom, Bob and Alfred, ended up working for the paper. Alfred was the youngest and only worked temporarily for his father, perhaps learning the trade, before moving to the *Northern Whig* in 1892. He was to become the editor of the *Northern Standard* in Monaghan.

James Troy joined the *Chronicle* as a young man in 1876 and worked his way up to the position of compositor in 1884, a role which had him laying out the pages of type to be printed up. By the time of his death in 1909, he had become the paper's foreman. His youngest son, Samuel Selfridge Troy (probably named after his mother, whose maiden name was Selfridge), married one Susan McBride and in 1935 they bought the *Chronicle*. They went on to have three sons: Robert J took over the running of the *Chronicle*, the *Coleraine Constiution* and the *Ballymena Guardian* with his brother, also Samuel Selfridge, while their other brother, Cyril, ended up working for Ulster Television.

A second paper also appeared later, in 1875, the *Coleraine Constitution*, which was managed and edited by J H Simms. Its name was changed to the *Northern Constitution* in 1967.

The Written Word

By the time that the bookstore chain Waterstone's had opened its doors in Coleraine—first on the campus of the University of Ulster on Cromore Road, and later on Church Street—it was nearly a quarter of a century after what was possibly the first bookstore had opened for business in the town, in 1762. The proprietor was William Mitchell, who had come from Belfast to set up his bookselling and binding business on the Diamond. A later bookseller in the area was David Dunlop, whose father, Captain William Dunlop, was to be hanged in Coleraine for his part in the 1798 Rising. This might be one reason behind David eventually leaving his home town for Sydney, Australia, where he died in 1863. Thanks to the Ordnance Survey, which was carried out during the 1830s, we have a record of the sort of magazines and periodicals that Mr Dunlop was selling in 1834. While a couple of women's magazines (*Magazine of Fashion*, *World Fashion*) are named alongside a large selection of religious titles (*Christian Ladies Magazine*, *Christian Guardian/Observer/Remembrancer/Examiner*,

Evangelical Magazine, *Family Sermons*), a lot of the periodicals and books were concerned with the acquirement of facts, particularly in the areas of medicine and general knowledge. For instance some customers were buying *Cyclopaedia of Medicine*, *Library of Useful Knowledge*, *Edinburgh Medical Journal*, *Dublin Medical Journal*, and *Johnson Medico*, while the monthly editions of *Penny Cyclopaedia*, *Laidum Cyclopaedia* and *Encyclopaedia Britannica* were quite popular. Apart from fashion and religion, hobbies being catered for in the regular purchases from Mr Dunlop's shelves included mechanics, sport and nature. Dunlop's biggest sellers were the *Penny Journal* and *Penny Magazine*; he sold thirty copies of each a month.

There are also records of another local bookseller, a Mr Hardy, for the same year. His biggest seller was the *Irish Penny Magazine*, with others like the *London Penny Magazine*, *Saturday Magazine*, *Chambers' Journals* and *Edinburgh Review* showing steady sales.

A third bookseller, Mr John Robinson, seemed to specialise in religious products. His periodicals were sent to him from their publishers in Belfast and his sales were generally greater than both Dunlop's and Hardy's, suggesting that his customers were cut from the same cloth, and knew him well. For instance:

Christian Freeman	sold 10 copies every month
Temperance Advocate	sold 20 copies every month
Orthodox Presbyterian	sold 22 copies every month
Sabbath School Magazine	sold 40 copies every month
Presbyterian Penny Magazine	sold 64 copies every month
Christian Gleaner	sold 60 copies every month
Friend of Youth	sold 32 copies every month

Aside from the *Christian Gleaner* (Canada's first 'disciple magazine'), which Mr Hardy sold just six copies of every month,

Mr Robinson appears to have been the exclusive supplier of his other religious titles.

For those who could not afford to spend money on periodicals and books, there was always the library which was established in 1806 and thrived on annual subscriptions of £1'1s. Dr Thomas Reid was both secretary and treasurer, and there were five others on the committee, Mr Robert Sharpe, Mr Robert Dallas, Rev William Sillito, Rev John Whiteside and Mr Robert Given. A room was provided rent free by the Corporation at the Corporation Hall and there was just one librarian, Joseph Matthews, who earned an annual wage of £5'10s. Six years earlier a newsroom was set up in the Town Hall where folk could keep up with current events via the local newspapers that were at hand. Titles included the *London Standard*, the *London Evening Mail*, the *Dublin Evening Mail*, the *Dublin Evening Post*, the *Liverpool Standard*, the *Belfast Chronicle*, the *Derry Sentinel*, the *Glasgow Herald*, and the *Navy and Army List*.

In 1929, a local woman, Mrs McElfatrick, was in her ninety-first year when she was interviewed by a reporter from the *Northern Constitution* about her earliest memories of Coleraine. She remembered, as a young girl, seeing the noble lady Mrs Maxwell, from Jackson Hall, who travelled in style and was presumably something of a reader. She would arrive at the book and stationery shop opposite the Town Hall in her carriage drawn by four bay horses, complete with coachmen and livery. This was also the same shop where Mrs McElfatrick and her friends bought their school books, and at that time it was run by a woman and her two daughters. Perhaps the woman was Mrs Anne Ward, who ran her own bookshop at the Diamond. She also published the *Coleraine Almanac* and wrote a few books of her own. Unfortunately, not much information survives about her today. However, she was related to the Marcus Ward who set up his successful printing/stationery shop in Belfast (*see* **Famous Connections**) and then became mother-in-law to the famous war correspondent, Charles Williams (*see* **Famous Connections**), who married her daughter Georgina. Following the death of her husband, Mrs Ward emigrated to California where she died in a freak drowning accident in 1873.

Jackson Hall

This was one of the grand old houses of Coleraine, built by Clotheworkers' tenants, the Jackson family, as far back as 1680. The first inhabitant was William Jackson. After that it appears the house was leased out; there are contracts dating from 1735 which directs tenants on the estate to bring their own turf to the mansion house every summer. William's descendent, Richard, had an extension built on to the house just before 1752. The house then became known as Jackson Hall when Janet Innes, Richard's aunt, lived there with her nephew. She died in 1763 and Richard had lots of construction work done on the house in the 1770s, which was probably long overdue as it was almost a century old by this stage. Thirty years later and Richard's son, George, could no longer afford to stay in the house, which was both sad and full of irony, considering that it was his father who had built it up to be a big, expensive residence, probably imagining his future bloodline residing there in comfort and splendour. George left for the south of England, selling his lease to T K Hannynton.

There is a brief description of the house at this time which refers to the fact that the hall and staircase had stands for several hundred guns, which would have been used to protect the tenants. Undoubtedly, the trouble and strife that attended the ambitions of United Irishmen in 1798—basically to do away with the upper classes—and resulted in gangs wandering throughout Coleraine and the north of Ireland, was still uppermost in people's minds. Hannynton had his agent look into making the front entrance to

Town Hall, Coleraine.

Town Hall, Coleraine.

Wreaths laid at the War Memorial, Coleraine.

War Memorial, Coleraine.

The fallen from the First World War.

The fallen from the Second World War.

St Patrick's Church, Coleraine.

Stained glass windows of St Patrick's Church, Coleraine.

The strand at Portrush.

White Rocks, Portrush.

the house a lot bigger, but went bankrupt before his plans could be implemented. The grounds surrounding the house were admired for the selection of ornamental trees which adorned them—these underwent a brutal culling by Hannynton's creditors, along with several smaller trees that were cut down by strangers and floated down the river on the estate. For years after, the house stood empty, uncared for and unloved until the arrival of Mrs Maxwell who, in 1824, leased the house for the next few years. Did she fall in love with the noble wreck as soon as she saw it, and how come she ended up in Coleraine in the first place? All that is said of her is that she was wealthy, and indeed, Jackson Hall flourished again, thanks to its new tenant spending over £2,000 on repairs on the house and grounds. The grove was blooming once more with new ornamental trees and all was right with the world.

However, nothing lasts forever. In a letter written in 1877 by a Maria Griffith to Mrs Knox, the author bemoans the fact that the house, a 'beautiful old site of ancient times', had undergone many changes that had been inflicted on it by a succession of tenants, including Mrs Knox's Uncle Charles who had had new, and different, windows put in; he had also divided the house up into different compartments. It was certainly the site of a romantic story: a Miss Jackson married her brother's tutor, the Reverend Nat Alexander, future Bishop of Meath, beneath one of the trees.

Jackson Hall later became known as Manor House and was sold to the Coleraine Council by Daniel Hall Christie, who was an MP from 1933 to 1937, and Chairman of Londonderry County Council. Soon after, the Council built County Hall and Coleraine Health Centre on its grounds.

The Water of Life
The word 'whiskey' actually comes from the Irish term 'uisce beatha' which is the translation of the Latin 'aqua vitae', which

means 'water of life'. This spirit, from distilled fermented cereals, has long been a part of the heritage of this island, though no one knows actually when it appeared. Ironically it seems that it might have been introduced by monks, because of its 'alleged' excellent healing properties; it is these properties that are the subject of a fourteenth century report. In fact, there is an old Irish proverb: 'What butter and whiskey cannot cure, there is no cure for' ('An té nach leigheasann im nó uiscc beatha, ní aon leigheas ar'). One would assume, however, that the monks advocated only drinking moderately for a cure; they surely would have shrugged their shoulders in disdain when a fifteenth century lord's passing was recorded in the annals, with an immoderate consumption of whiskey being named as the primary cause of death. Obviously the popularity of the spirit was growing; so much so that in 1556, the Irish Parliament highlighted their concern that the 'water of life' was being made all over Ireland in order to keep up with the demand of a population who seemed to be imbibing daily. Their concern was two-fold: the amount of valuable grain which was being used for whiskey and also, naturally, the effect the drink was having on the rate of crime. A solution was duly found and a law was passed which stated that a licence was now required to distil.

A licence to distil was granted on 20 April 1608 to Sir Thomas Phillips, for the 'Countie of Colrane', and the famous Bushmills Distillery was born.

In 1755 Coleraine, as a distillery town, was second only to Dublin, raising £1,267 in excise duties against Dublin's £4,993. When times were good in the 1750s distilleries thrived both in Coleraine and Killowen, which was linked to Coleraine by a ferry and then a bridge, but there is nothing permanent in business. In 1776 worries about the availability of foodstuffs resulted in the appearance of a letter in the *Belfast News Letter* in which Coleraine and Kilrea distillers promised to do everything they could to stop the poor from undergoing any suffering that might be caused by the scarcity of grain, caused in turn by the production of whiskey. Accordingly they were going to refrain from using anything other than barley and bere until the next harvest. Then, three years later, thanks to the 1779 Distilling Act and the growing popularity/accessibility of that commoner fuel, poteen (poitín), sales slackened resulting in distilleries being forced to close their doors. The situation was pretty grim at the turn of the century but then, in 1820, John Rennie converted a mill in Newmarket Street into a distillery.

The 1779 Distilling Act brought in new taxes for distillers: the amount they had to pay was based on the stills capacity and throughput, which is the amount of produce that was processed. Not surprisingly the stringent new levies led to a dramatic decrease in the number of licensed distillers, while there was an equally dramatic increase in the number of unlicensed distillers. Apparently Donegal became a sort of hot bed for illegally produced whiskey and, by 1822, there was thought to be something in the region of eight hundred unlicensed stills spewing out untaxed poteen, or 'moonshine', as it became known.

Newmarket Street was a relatively new street in Coleraine. It used to be called Boyd Street, after Dr John Boyd, a well known character (*see* **Famous Connections**) in the town. Nine years after Rennie converted his mill the Corporation built a new market-place, hence the name. The street became synonymous with taking a break from the day's business. It was littered with drinking houses which were frequented by farmers, dealers and market folk, who also made use of the stables out back. For instance, if lengthy negotiations were required to properly price a horse then it made sense to have the animal fed and brushed down while buyer and seller adjourned to the bar for a wee tipple and further discussion. This was how Dirty Lane got its name; it would have been where the stables were cleaned out.

Nobody is exactly sure who bought Rennie's brand new distillery but, in 1837, Thomas Black was marketing Coleraine Whiskey. (Maybe this was the same Thomas Black, whose eldest daughter, Anne, married Francis Ward, from the Coleraine paper-mills' family. Anne went on to open a bookshop on the Diamond in 1852.) He sold the business the following year to Michael Ferrar, who ran it for the next eleven years, before selling it on to James Moore in 1848. By all accounts Ferrar did a good job and was soon supplying whiskey to the bar in the House of Commons, of all places. The Coleraine bottle became famous for its 'House of Commons' or 'HC' label.

Business continued to improve under James Moore, so much so that he was able to build a brewery at Brook Street and a maltings at Tullans. (For the uninitiated, when barley or wheat grains have been soaked in water for two or three days and then allowed to sprout before being dried out in a kiln, this is known as a malt. Therefore, a maltings is where a grain is made into malt.) Moore died in 1868 and fellow businessman/merchant Robert Taylor stepped in, buying both the distillery and the maltings. The Brook Street brewery was the possession of George Topp, and Taylor had to wait until 1871 to buy it after Topp went bankrupt. A successful and intelligent businessman, Taylor was very fond of the distillery and only the most experienced men were hired to work in it. The politicians in the House of Commons continued to enjoy Coleraine Whiskey and the business blossomed. Taylor added a bottling plant in the late 1880s, and an entirely new concept was born when the single malt was matured for ten years. (A single malt whiskey is where a whiskey made from a single type of malted grain is distilled at a single distiller.) In other words the amount of whiskey produced each year was relatively small, only 100,000 gallons a year.

The rarity of the whiskey was probably a factor in its success.

Following an inspection, the distillery was passed with flying colours, branded as the cleanest and most efficient in the whole country. When Robert Taylor died in 1902 his nephew, Andrew Clarke, took over. Unfortunately, the business suffered as a result and, following a lengthy struggle, the distillery shut down in the 1920s. It stood empty until it was bought by William Boyd four years before the outbreak of the Second World War, in 1935. Whiskey was in his blood, so to speak; his father Samuel had bought the Bushmills distillery in 1923 and turned it into a success. William made a second purchase a couple of years later when he bought the recently developed Killowen distillery to use it as a bonded warehouse (where goods on which taxes are unpaid are stored under bond) for Bushmills and Coleraine whiskey.

Just after the Second World War, in 1946, the Boyds sold their interests in their two distilleries to Isaac Wolfson of Great Universal Stores (GUS), which resulted in massive changes: from now on, all the malting would be done at Bushmills while all the bottling would take place at Coleraine. All the GUS whiskey would now be branded under the one name, Bushmills, including the bottles.

Today there are two 'Coleraine whiskeys': a single malt, the Coleraine 34, and a blended malt of whiskey and grain from Bushmills. According to Brian Townsend's book, *The Lost Distilleries of Ireland*, there were some 395 bottles of the Coleraine 34 knocking about in 1999 that had been distilled in the old Newmarket distillery in 1959—although most sold for £300 as soon as they appeared on the market. Nowadays, this particular whiskey is a bit more expensive. One collectors' website, at the time of writing, was selling a bottle of Coleraine 34 on behalf of an anonymous client, and the asking price was £1,400! As Townsend says, the 1959 bottle is a lasting tribute to what is generally perceived as one of the greatest lost distilleries in this country.

Road Racers

Coleraine is part of one of the most famous triangles in the world;
that is, within the world of motorcycle racing. The circuit of the
North West 200 race, between Portrush, Portstewart and Coleraine,
is thought to be one of the fastest in the world, where speeds of
200mph have been reached. In fact, Michael Rutter, a British rider,
smashed this record in 2005, ratcheting up a speed of 201.1mph.
The North West is among the most widely attended events across
the UK and Ireland. In 2006 a massive 150,000 spectators from
Ireland, Britain and Europe turned up to cheer on the brave riders
from the side of the roads. The race, which had been run since
1929, passes private houses on the outskirts of the three towns,
which means that some preparation is required; for instance, all the
street signs are removed and bales of hay are wrapped around
immovable objects, such as lampposts and telegraph posts, and
corner boards have to be erected. An enormous painting and
decorating job is also implemented, with brake lines being painted
on the road, and all the kerbs receiving a coat or two also. There is
an army of personnel on the day itself, with over seven hundred
marshals, medical, fire control and communications staff.

There are two practice runs before the big day, on the Tuesday
and Thursday. Then, on the Saturday, the public roads are closed
for the afternoon and the racing commences. The original 'North
West 200' was a two hundred-mile circuit, but nowadays it is six
separate races, each running four to six laps of the 8.966 mile
circuit, 8.83 miles on the first lap of every race.

The competition is fierce, with the crème de la crème of world-
class riders turning up to try their luck. Of course, the race is
synonymous with the two Dunlop brothers from the area: Joey was
victorious thirteen times before his untimely death in 2000, while
racing in Estonia; his younger brother, Robert, with fifteen wins
under his belt, was the most successful rider on the circuit—

unfortunately, he too died, on 15 May 2008, while practicing for his race in the 250cc class, during the 125/250/400cc session. At a speed of 160mph the bike seized, sending Robert over the handlebars and colliding with fellow rider, Darren Burns, who was immediately behind him. Both the brothers' funerals were attended by huge crowds, a testament to their popularity and their talent. The contribution they made to the promotion of the sport in Northern Ireland, and, in particular, to the North West 200 cannot be underestimated.

It is not just the roar of the motorbikes that brings the crowds; the race has developed into a proper festival with plenty of highlights to attract families and fans. There are lots of things to see: vintage cars, arena trials, stunt riders with nerves of steel, aeroplanes, supermotos, and even grass track races, as well as the extra-curricular activities laid on by the Coleraine and Ballymoney Borough Councils. The forerunner of today's event came about back in the 1920s when the City of Derry and District Motor Club wanted to host 'a big event'. The fantastic idea of having a two hundred-mile road race was touted and the organisers set about finding a circuit within the region of Londonderry, approximately five miles from the city. The name of the race would be the North West 200, owing to the location. Some hurried consultation took place between Coleraine, Portrush and Portstewart representatives, who came up with the triangular course and invited the club committee to hear their proposals. Their offer of the circuit was promptly accepted and, because the committee was so gracious about moving the venue, the representatives from the three towns insisted that the name remain the North West 200.

Saturday, 20 April 1929 was the date of the very first race, when, as was the norm, the riders were given a handicap, starting at different intervals. Three 'limit men' set off at 1pm with the most generous handicap, followed by the rest of their competitors over

the next hour, the last two riders, the 'scratch men', finally hitting
the road at 1.53pm. The route was the road from Coleraine to
Portrush and it was a much slower race than it is today. Coleraine
man, Malcolm McQuigg, was the first rider to complete the second
lap, eventually coming second on a 246cc Zenith, finishing the
race, with his handicap of fifty-one minutes, in three hours, thirty-
nine minutes and fifty seconds. He won the Portstewart Cup and a
whopping £2 for making the fastest time in the 250cc class.

List of the Multiple Winners

Wins

15	Robert Dunlop		
13	Joey Dunlop		
12	Michael Rutter		
11	Phillip McCallen		
09	Tony Rutter	Ian Lougher	
06	Bruce Anstey	Steve Cull	
05	Ian Simpson	Arthur Wheeler	
	John Williams	Mick Grant	
	Woolsey Coulter	Steve Plater	
04	Bob McIntyre	David Jeffries	Jimmy Guthrie
	Ernie Nott	Eddie Laycock	Tommy Robb
03	Alan Shepherd	Artie Bell	Callum Ramsey
	Geoff Duke	Charlie Williams	Jim Moodie
	Eric Fernihough	Ralph Bryans	Ray McCullough
	Rod Gould	Trevor Nation	Tom Herron
	Sammy Miller		
02	Alistair King	Andy Watts	Bob Anderson
	Carl Fogarty	Charlie Manders	John 'Crasher' White
	Dave Leach	Derek Chatterton	Derek Ennett
	Donnie Robinson	Fred Stevens	Gary Cowan

Graham Wood   Ian Newton   Jack Brett
John Blanchard   John Cooper   Kevin Mitchell
Peter Williams   Phelim Owens   Dick Creith
Robert Holden   Roger Marshall   Ryan Farquhar
Steve Hislop   Percy 'Tim' Hunt   Walter Rusk
Jack Brett

PART TWO
FAMOUS CONNECTIONS

James Johnston Abraham (1876-1963)

was born in Coleraine. Upon finishing secondary school he left his hometown for Trinity College in Dublin to study medicine. His fist professional appointment took him to County Clare and then in 1908 he was made Resident Medical Officer to the London Dock Hospital and Rescue Home. At the outbreak of war in 1914 Abraham applied to join the Royal Army Medical Corps (RAMC); however, his application was turned down because he was deemed to be too senior, which allowed the Red Cross mission to benefit from his expertise. They welcomed him into their ranks via Sir Frederick Treves, a famous surgeon at the time.

The following year Abraham found himself even further from home when he was given charge of the first Red Cross Serbian Mission. His task was a challenging one. Serbia was a poor country with few medical facilities. Dreadful overcrowding led to inadequate sanitary conditions which, in turn, led inevitably to the spread of disease. The already fierce strain on meagre medical supplies was truly exacerbated by the onslaught of small pox and scarlet fever, not to mention the typhus epidemic of 1915.

Abraham writes with clarity about attempting to deal with this particularly devastating disease in his autobiography, *Surgeon's Journey*. In fact he was the first doctor on location to diagnose typhus. Following the initial outbreak the authorities tried to hide the fact that the virus was utterly rampant. There was no cure in

1915 and the mortality rate for patients under the age of fifty was approximately twenty per cent, while the rate of deaths for the over-fifties was fifty per cent. When the fifty-year-old Dr R O Cooke arrived from London to offer his services, Abraham felt obliged to risk offence by turning the consultant away because of his potentially dangerous age. The eminent doctor left him in a huff and, determined to be of use, went straight to the Serb authorities who gave him the run of the Polymesis Hospital, where two doctors had recently died of typhus. Three weeks later Abraham visited Cooke at his new work place, perhaps with the intention of salvaging a friendship, where to his dismay—but not surprise—he found him in a delirious state. He immediately took the doctor back to his own hospital and, fortunately, was able to make him well again. The only consequence of the experience, for Cooke, was that he had no memory of the previous month; furthermore, when he bumped into Abraham years later, in London, he could not remember having met him, never mind having been saved by him. Amnesia is a common occurrence with the disease.

Abraham recognised that Serbia was in the grip of a dreadful epidemic, an inevitable companion of war when food and medicine were rationed, and cramped life on the battlefield was far from clean and proper. It is believed that the typhus started with the Austrian prisoners who began to die, literally in their thousands. Then the civilian population of Serbia caught it, with the result that people arrived at the hospitals in their hundreds, thereby bringing the disease to the attending—and over-worked—doctors and nurses, many of whom also perished. This meant that victims were forced to stay at home, dying unattended by medical practitioners. Others jumped on trains to escape the virus but they succumbed en route to the south. Abraham writes that people were dying in the streets, guessing that well over a million had been infected.

The symptoms were a rocketing temperature, vomiting, headache and painful limbs, with a rash of red spots usually appearing on the fifth day. The patient simultaneously experienced a drowsiness which progressed to a sometimes violent delirium.

At that point the cause of the disease was unknown but by the time that Abraham was writing his story it had been discovered that typhus was carried by lice. He reckoned that he and his colleague, Banks, escaped infection thanks to their compulsion to lather themselves several times a day with a mixture of Vaseline and paraffin oil, specifically to keep the lice away.

By the time his contract with the Red Cross was up Abraham and his five orderlies (all that was left out of twelve) were ready to leave. There actually was an option for the team to renew their contract and stay a bit longer but not one of them had any intention of staying on, and understandably so, considering the stress and strain of their situation. The Coleraine man had lost four stone and was almost burnt out. His next appointment took him to the Middle East before he returned to London to take up a specialist position in Harley Street. He was made a Knight of St John Consulting Surgeon at the Princess Beatrice Hospital in London. Later on he became a Fellow of the Royal Society of Medicine, and President of the Irish Medical Graduate's Association, winning their Arnott Medal in 1949, the same year he received an Honorary Doctorate.

His *Surgeon's Journal; Balkan Log and The Surgeon's Log* was reprinted thirty times.

John Bodkin Adams (1899-1983)

Adams was actually born in Randalstown. His father, Samuel, was a watchmaker who married Ellen Bodkin in 1896. The family moved to Ballinderry Bridge in County Tyrone where young Adams attended the local Methodist day school. Then, in 1911, the family moved to Ebenezer House, Mount Sandel, Coleraine, to allow Adams to attend Coleraine Academical Institution. Samuel died of a stroke in 1914 when Adams was at the vulnerable age of fifteen years, and this was followed four years later by the death of his only sibling, younger brother William, who died in the worldwide influenza pandemic of 1918. (There is no exact number for the victims of this particular pandemic, which has been described as 'the greatest medical holocaust in history', but experts estimate that somewhere between forty and one hundred million succumbed, with the virus—more commonly known as the 'Spanish Lady'—even reaching the Arctic and remote Pacific Islands.) Adams enrolled at Queen's University Belfast to study medicine, graduating in 1921, but failing to achieve any honours, having missed at least a year when he was struck down with tuberculosis. He didn't have many friends and was mostly a bit of a loner.

The year he left college he was offered a position as houseman at Bristol Royal Infirmary where he spent the next twelve months. This involved performing minor operations while also assisting the registrar and consultant with the more serious procedures. However, the job didn't really suit him, so on his boss's advice, he applied to a Christian practice in Eastbourne which was looking for a general practitioner. His application was a success and, in 1922, he moved to Eastbourne to share a house with his mother and cousin, Florence Henry. The next few years passed and it can be assumed that the young man looked forward to having his own home, and not just any old home. In 1929 he borrowed £2,000 from William Mawhood, a wealthy patient of his. The massive loan allowed him to purchase Kent Lodge, a house with no less than eighteen rooms, in Trinity Trees. The story goes that for the next twenty years, until William's death in 1949, Adams was constantly in the company of the Mawhoods, continually turning up at mealtimes, and inviting himself as well as his mother and cousin to their dinner table. On top of that Adams began frequenting local shops and charging items to the Mawhood account. After William's passing, Adams visited his widow and left with a twenty-two carat gold pen that was sitting on her bedside table, telling her he wanted a keepsake of her husband. She never saw him again, and later described him as 'a real scrounger' when she was interviewed by the police.

In 1935 Adams inherited £7,385 from another patient, Mrs Matilda Whitton. Her entire estate was worth £11,465; therefore, her doctor's share was wildly greater than any of her blood relatives' slices of the wealth. They naturally contested the will but it was upheld in court.

Adams remained in Eastbourne during the war years and it is notable that he was not invited to join the 'pool system', whereby doctors would treat the patients of those colleagues who had left to fight Hitler, which might suggest that his reputation as a general practitioner was not particularly good among his peers. Nevertheless, he persevered with his chosen profession and, in 1941, gained a diploma in anaesthetics. He worked one day a week in a local hospital and once again the impression is that his efficiency was severely lacking. It was said that he fell asleep during operations, and would be preoccupied by eating or even counting money, which may explain how he kept mixing up the anaesthetic gas tubes. This meant that some patients who didn't receive enough anaesthetic would wake up during their operations—an upsetting prospect for both surgeon and patient—while others who didn't require as much would turn blue from over-dosage.

His mother died in 1943, and was spared from witnessing the horrific turn of events in 1956.

Over the next thirteen years or so rumours circulated about Adams' incompetence and all-round strange little quirks as a doctor. For instance, he would ask nurses to leave the room before he would treat a patient with one of his 'special injections' and, invariably, he would fail to communicate exactly to the nursing staff what the injections contained. There was also the alarming fact that an incredible 132 patients mentioned him in their wills. In eleven years, between 1944 and 1955, he 'made' £21,600 out of fourteen legacies. This sort of thing naturally resulted in the good doctor becoming the subject of much gossip. And perhaps it was all just speculation. Whatever about his technical abilities, it must be said that his bedside manner was rated top-notch, particularly with the female of the species. His practice was quite a lucrative one all round as he was the definite favourite with the many elderly patients who had retired to the south coast.

Then, on 23 July 1956, the Eastbourne police received an anonymous call about the death of one Gertrude Hullett, who had been a patient of Adams. When she died unexpectedly, her friend Leslie Henson, a music hall performer, rang the police with his suspicions. Gertrude was only fifty years old and in a deep depression following the death of her husband, Alfred John, four months earlier. The seventy-one-year-old Mr Hullett was also a patient of Adams and had kindly left his doctor £500 in his will. The facts are a little ambiguous concerning Gertrude's death. As stated, she was very depressed and confided in Adams her wish to kill herself. He prescribed sodium barbitone and sodium phenobarbitone for her depression and insomnia, which she took in large amounts. It is generally believed that she took an overdose on 19 July and was in a coma when she was discovered the next morning. Adams couldn't get to her house until later that day so she was administered to by a Dr Harris. For some reason Adams didn't tell his colleague about Gertrude's depression or her prescribed medication, and instead agreed with the doctor's diagnosis, based on the patient's contracted pupils, that she may have suffered a cerebral haemorrhage. On 20 July, when the pathologist asked if he should examine the contents of Gertrude's stomach to check for narcotic poisoning, both Doctors Harris and Adams told him it wasn't necessary. The results of a urine sample were delivered after Gertrude died; she had 115 grains of sodium barbitone in her body, twice the fatal dose.

At the inquest which followed, the coroner queried why an overdose was never considered by her long-term doctor. As it happened Adams eventually, on 22 July, raised the possibility of barbiturate poisoning and asked a colleague for guidance but it was too late by then. There was also the matter that Adams delayed in giving his patient oxygen just hours before she died, despite a nurse describing her as blue. The nurse also described the patient as 'sweating a good deal' for the last three days of her life, yet when the coroner asked Adams why he had not given Gertrude an intravenous drip, he replied that it hadn't been necessary since she wasn't perspiring at all. In the end the inquest decided that Gertrude had committed suicide, and the coroner instructed the jury against finding Adams guilty of criminal negligence.

Meanwhile Gertrude, in a will that was drawn up just nine days before her overdose, left Adams her 1954 Rolls Royce Silver Dawn. Six days before her death, she had given her doctor a cheque for £1,000. He took it to the bank on 18 July and, on being told that it would only be cleared by 21 July, he asked for it to be 'specially cleared', which would mean his account would be credited on 19 July. This system was usually only required if a customer had reason to believe a cheque was going to bounce, but Gertrude Hullett was one of the richest women in Eastbourne. Strangely enough, that cheque disappeared during the police investigation.

The Hulletts' case was the straw that broke the camel's back but, six years earlier, there had been the peculiarities surrounding the medical treatment of wealthy widow, Edith Alice Morrell. She had moved to Eastbourne in 1948 after suffering a stroke which had left her partially paralysed and with severe arthritis. Dr Adams treated her with concoctions of heroin and morphine to help her sleep. In fact his dosages were rather alarming, a fact which was only discovered later. The eighty-one-year-old died on 13 November 1950 from, according to her doctor, another stroke.

She had made several wills during the last two years of her life, some of which granted her doctor large sums of money and furniture, and others which didn't mention him at all. Finally, on 24 August 1949, she made an addition to her last will, a codicil which stated that Dr Adams was to receive nothing from her estate. Nevertheless, when she died, despite the codicil, he managed to 'receive' her Rolls Royce Silver Ghost and a set of silver cutlery, worth about £276, that he had long admired. As if that wasn't enough, he took an infra-red lamp that Mrs Morrell had bought herself for £60 and installed it at his surgery. The police found that although he had visited his patient approximately 321 times he had actually charged the estate for 1,100 visits, to the tune of £1,674.

There was no post-mortem. Adams had her cremated on the very same day she died, filling out a form which claimed that he had no financial interest in Mrs Morrell's death. Later that evening her ashes were scattered over the English Channel. The evidence, as it were, was gone forever. Yet it was the death of Mrs Morrell that landed Dr Adams on trial at the Old Bailey in 1957. You can imagine the amount of gossip by the time that Gertrude Hullett drew her last breath. A local newspaper carried the heading 'Inquiry into 400 Wills' and there was also a poem by an anonymous author (later believed to be a Fleet Street journalist) which stated that if you wanted your rich relatives bumped off, send them to Eastbourne for a 'Bodkin speciality'. The police were virtually bound to start an investigation due to the persistent demands of the Eastbourne population. By the time they arrested

Adams, on 19 December 1956, he was one of the richest doctors in England. His reaction on being read his rights was 'Murder...murder... Can you prove it was murder? She was dying at any rate.' This didn't look too good.

The trial lasted seventeen days, a first in British legal history. Dr John Bodkin Adams was tried initially for the murder of Mrs Morrell, with the case for the murder of Gertrude Hullett to be heard afterwards. Incredibly, Adams was acquitted. He knew a lot of powerful men who may or may not have pulled a few strings for him. There was even a journalist's memo found by the police which strongly suggested that Dr Adams was having an affair with one of those powerful men, a magistrate no less.

That missing cheque from Gertude Hullett, for instance, was only one of several 'conveniences' that saved Adams from the death penalty or life imprisonment. Another major factor was the discovery—too late—of the previously mislaid nurses' notebook which recorded all the injections that Adams had administered to Edith Alice Morrell. Up to that point all that was available were the replies, during cross-examination, of the four nurses who took care of the patient and who had withheld their personal concerns over the quantities and frequency of the injections; the notebook, when produced, contradicted any of their 'accidental' exaggerations. Furthermore, some of the police subordinates were astounded that Mrs Morrell's death was to be the primary charge, considering that her body was now particles of dust surfing the waves across the English Channel. There had been plenty of other cases to choose from, where actual bodies could have been tested for narcotic poisoning.

The jury found Adams not guilty in less than forty-five minutes on 15 April 1957. Immediately after the trial he resigned from the National Health Service. His troubles weren't over though: a few months later he was fined £2,400 for forging prescriptions, making false statements on cremation forms, and for three offences under the Dangerous Drugs Act 1951. On 22 November he was struck off the Medical Register, only to be reinstated in 1961. It would seem that his colleagues did not think he was a killer, and they weren't the only ones. A lot of people believed that he merely helped sick, elderly people who had already voiced their wish to die. It just happened that his clients were wealthy and much inclined to leave him a gift in exchange for his help. He told one colleague that he accepted legacy receipts in place of fees as he had no use for money. There were others, of course, who never doubted that he preyed on the wealthy and the elderly, killing them over time with lethal doses of drugs. These people, including police officials and at least one of his old friends, believed that he had brought about the deaths of 163 of his patients. Whatever you choose to believe, Adams received legacies right up until his own death in 1983. When he died his estate was worth £402,970.

William Allingham (1824-1889)

Allingham was born in Ballyshannon, County Donegal on 19 March, the eldest of five children. His father was a bank manager and obviously advocated it as a career of choice for his son. Upon leaving school Allingham reluctantly followed his parents' advice and took a banking job. This was soon followed by a job in customs which meant a move to Coleraine, in 1846, to take up the position of Controller of Customs. Perhaps he was anxious to make a strike for independence from his family, and find a way of getting out of Donegal. His father, however, would not have been able to fault his new job and might have perceived it as a worthy substitution to working in a bank. In any case, as far as William was concerned, the job was a means to an end as his first love was writing poetry.

William's home in Coleraine was the Customs House, at the corner of Bridge Street and Circular Road Junction, which was built in 1783 as a result of the growing importance of the Port of Coleraine, by the Board of Customs, whose property it remained although some dispute arose between the Board and the Irish Society who claimed the site as their own and wanted the House moved to another.

Between 1830 and 1838 a series of articles and information was collected on Coleraine by the Department of Ordnance, to accompany the new maps that had been drawn and printed. In this way we have a picture, and a damning one, of the Customs House, and this would have been before young William arrived to take up his post. The house was described as being small and in a bit of a state. It was barely being held together by iron bars which were apparent throughout the building, going in every direction.

We may assume that he was an avid reader of his contemporaries; he regularly visited London and had made contact with the likes of Lord Alfred Tennyson, Leigh Hunt and Thomas Carlyle. He also kept a diary of his life which was filled with the cultural goings-on of nineteenth century Britain.

His first volume of *Poems* was published in 1850, and dedicated to Hunt. This was followed four years later by a second volume, *Day and Night Songs*, which included 'The Music Master' about the parting of two lovers. The book was published to great acclaim, and it was illustrated by Pre-Raphaelite painters Dante Gabriel Rossetti and John Everett Millais when it was reissued the following year. Allingham applied for a transfer in the Customs Service and moved to Hampshire in 1863, settling within a stone's throw from the Tennyson residence. Aside from writing his own poetry he started to collect ballads that could be bought on the street. He compiled and edited a book of these ballads and had it published in 1864. That same year he published his long narrative poem, 'Laurence Bloomfield in Ireland', about the struggle between landlords and tenants, to great acclaim. The Russian novelist and playwright Ivan

Turgenev wrote that he had never understood Ireland until he read the poem while William Gladstone quoted from it at Westminster. Allingham also became interested in composing songs for children, his most famous being 'The Fairies'. In 1865 his *Fifty Modern Poems* collection was published.

Five years later his good friend Thomas Carlyle helped him to make the decision to leave the safety of the Customs Service after twenty-four years to start work as a sub-editor with *Fraser's Magazine*. He was now forty-six years old. He finally married, at the age of fifty, the twenty-six-year-old painter Helen Paterson in 1874. They had two sons and a daughter and their marriage was a happy one. He must have been a sociable man as he continued to befriend all the big names in the world of letters, writers like Charles Dickens, and Elizabeth and Robert Barret Browning.

When the editor of *Fraser's Magazine*, the historian J A Frode, retired in 1874 Allingham took over the post for the next five years. He and his family moved to Surrey in 1879 and then on to Hampstead, where he died on 18 November 1889. His diary, which he had written purely for his own enjoyment, was edited by his wife and published in 1907, proving him to be a talented and accurate recorder, along the lines of a James Boswell. In 1905 William Butler Yeats selected and edited a volume of Allingham's poetry, *Sixteen Poems*, referring to Allingham as 'my master in Irish verse'.

John Boyd (1789-1862)

Boyd was born at Bellisle, near Dervock, but moved to Coleraine when he was eleven years old. He became a larger-than-life character in the town and was full of flaws, as the best characters usually are. His career began with an apprenticeship to the local doctor, Dr James Thompson, and it was assumed that the student would succeed his mentor on the latter's retirement. Accordingly

Boyd went off to Glasgow to study medicine and, as soon as he graduated, he returned to the Thompson household to resume his work. Things went to plan on the elder doctor's retirement, albeit temporarily. Boyd ran the practice for two years and in that time professional distractions served to take up more and more of his time, which ultimately led to his abandoning medicine.

With the little information available it is hard to discern what sort of man Boyd was. He was either a very calculating individual, and was manipulative of people, or he was blessed with excellent social skills that served to make him a genuine and trustworthy friend. Thanks to his standing as a doctor he met and was liked by all the important people in Coleraine, who in turn, foisted well-paid public positions upon him. He was even hired as an agent for several landlords, which is certainly an indication of the regard in which he was held. He was both Mayor and Chamberlain of Coleraine more than once, which points to his general popularity in the town. He was also by this stage a landlord himself, after both buying and leasing land in and around the town from the Irish Society, amongst others.

More proof of his charismatic personality is to be found within a letter, dated 10 December 1842, by the MP for Coleraine, Edward Litton, who describes the ways in which Boyd was a rock of support. The former doctor canvassed for Litton's tenure as a local representative and was a loyal and constant friend to him. This support was rewarded by Litton's wholesale endorsement of Boyd when John became a Member of Parliament.

Boyd won the 1842 election by twenty-two votes and was doing so well financially that he was able to build his family a grand home, Dundooan House, which they moved into after the Christmas of 1844. His wife, Anna Arabella, was the daughter of the Reverend Robert Hezlett, the Rector of Killowen.

At one point Boyd held eleven positions in the town:

Chamberlain, Coroner, Bank Agent, Post Master, Tithe Collector and Evaluator, Commissioner of Oaths, Linen Seal Master, Town Clerk, Clerk of Records' Court, Clerk to Crown and Peace and, of course, his seat in Parliament.

He was in trouble a few years later; mounting debts brought pursuit through the courts with no less than five Queen's Bench judgements chasing his tail. Not surprisingly he withdrew from Parliament, and his seat went to Lord Naas. Further trouble brewed as it was believed by some that Lord Naas had had to buy the seat, an allegation hotly denied by Boyd. No matter, he returned to Coleraine and life went on. As it happens he was re-elected again in 1857. The following year, he began to cash in his property investments; he sold 545 acres at Ballyreagh, Slimague, Boghill, Ballysally, Spital Hill and Highlow Row. This continued into 1859 when he sold his residential properties in Coleraine and a hotel in Portrush.

He would only live for another three years. It seems that he liked to play as hard as he worked, and descriptions of him in his later years refer to him bearing the weary features of the hardened drinker. He also liked to gamble but, unfortunately, did not like to pay his debts, despite his huge wealth. One neighbour thought he was a true rogue who lived by his wits. However, there was no faulting the man in his professional capability. When he hung up his Chamberlain hat after thirty years of service all his accounts and paperwork were in perfect order.

His portrait hung in the new Town Hall after a campaign by the townsfolk. One fan had even written to the *Coleraine Chronicle* to remark upon the former mayor's genuine friendship with the ordinary people—no matter how grand or noble his companions were, he always stopped to greet and shake a person's hand if they were known to him. Boyd had watched the foundation stone being laid for the new building and told the excited crowd that he remembered standing beneath the arches of the old Market House over fifty years earlier, and whatever helped to improve Coleraine, aesthetically and administratively, was absolutely fine by him. Whatever else could be said about him, he had a deep love for Coleraine. When he was made MP again in 1859, he gave a speech about how much the town and its people meant to him, and how he wished to end his days there, which he duly did.

The *Coleraine Chronicle* published a description of his funeral in 1862; his hearse, which travelled from Dundooan House to Coleraine's parish church, had so many followers, from all walks of life, that the entire procession was over a mile long. Mourners included the Town Commissioners, the town's policemen in full uniform, along with the superintendent and the night constables.

Harry Gregg (b.1932)
Harry was born on 25 October in the village of Toberone, South Derry, but moved to Coleraine when he was a young boy. He grew up within 150 yards of the football stadium, a bit of an omen considering the direction his life was to take. Gregg was to become famous for two reasons, one of which was his goal-keeping abilities, which were world class.

When he left school he wanted to be a carpenter and got a job as a joiner earning the grand sum of £1 a week. Some accounts have him beginning his football career with Dundalk while others have him starting off by playing part-time with Windsor Park Swifts Football Club, Linfield's reserve team. Then he signed up with his local club, Coleraine FC, which had been founded just five years before Gregg was born. He was the goalie for that famous 1952 match against Glasgow Celtic in which the visitors won 2–0.

When he was eighteen years old he was approached by Doncaster Rovers and asked if he would like to join their squad. He answered in the positive and moved across the Irish Sea. Ninety-three games later, in December 1957, his wildest dreams were realised when the manager of Manchester United, Matt Busby, signed him up for a staggering £23,500, making him at that time the most expensive goalkeeper in the world. He made his debut in a match against Leicester City on 21 December 1957. It was his total dominance in the air that set him apart from his peers, his focus on the ball prompting him to jump for every cross, even if it meant that he, unintentionally, sent his own defenders sprawling.

Sir Alexander Matthew 'Matt' Busby (1909–1994) was born in a two-roomed miner's cottage in North Lanarkshire, Scotland. He lost his father and all his uncles in World War One and perhaps he relied on his passion for football to provide some comfort and support. He took over as manager of Manchester United at the beginning of 1946 and was to become the longest serving person in that role in the club's history. His first tenure lasted until 1969 and he returned to manage for the 1970-1971 season. With little experience at managing a team Busby's strategy was to gradually replace older players with much younger ones, some as young as sixteen. These talented young men became known as 'Busby's Babes', an affectionate jibe about their age.

The New Year of 1958 began very well and Gregg showed his worth with some spectacular work. The team played Red Star Belgrade at home in the European Cup tournament, winning 2-1, and followed this with a draw, 3-3, on Red Star's home turf. According to eyewitnesses the Manchester United goalie was the star of both matches. There were great celebrations after the Belgrade draw and the following day, 6 February, the team, in understandably high spirits, boarded the plane for home. Their British European Airways plane, called *Lord Burghley*, was the same aircraft that had taken them out to Belgrade that previous Monday and the journey home involved a brief stop in Germany for refuelling at the Riem Airport in Munich, where there was a heavy snowstorm. Apart from the 'Busby Babes', passengers included several British sports journalists and club officials; altogether there were thirty-eight passengers and six crew on board.

Apparently the pilot delayed taking off from Munich as he was unhappy about one of the engines and, indeed, there was some difficulty in getting the plane off the ground. It was on the third attempt to take off that the plane somehow overshot the runway and hit a house with one of its wings, causing it to veer in the other direction and hit another building before crashing to the ground and bursting into flames. Fortunately, the body of the plane, the fuselage, did not explode, and Gregg, who had just stumbled bleeding and bruised to relative safety on the runway with other unhurt passengers, was prompted to retrace his steps. Thus began the sequence of events which would explain the second reason for which Harry became famous, earning the mantle, 'The Hero of Munich', as a result. Gregg suddenly remembered there had been a baby on board and ran back into the burning wreck to look for it. At first he couldn't find twenty-two month old Venona Lukic; she wasn't on the seat where he had remembered seeing her. However, it was at that moment that the shocked infant chose to let out a cry and Gregg was able to pull her out from under the debris that covered her. He handed the child over to the flight's radio officer, George Rogers. He then went back in a second time to find Venona's mother, Vera, the pregnant wife of a Yugoslavian diplomat. Vera's legs were broken and she was suffering from a fractured skull, so Gregg was obliged to push her, using his feet, through a gap, which had ripped through the plane's body. When she had been taken to safety Gregg concentrated on his colleagues, pulling Bobby Charlton and Dennis Viollett out of the wreckage by their waistbands. He found his manager lying on the ground between the plane and the house it had struck; both his legs were broken and he had lost a good deal of blood. Then he located his friend Jackie Blanchflower, who had lost part of his arm. Gregg applied a tourniquet before bringing him to safety. All of this was achieved against a background of the constant threat that the plane would explode and kill everyone around it.

Twenty-one people died that night: eight young, talented footballers (Roger Byrne, Duncan Edwards, Eddie Colman, Mark Jones, Tommy Taylor, Liam Whelan, David Pegg and Geoff Bent), eight journalists, and three club officials, amongst others. The country was united in grief and even Queen Elizabeth professed to be 'deeply shocked', sending a message of condolence to the Lord Mayor of Manchester, and the Minister of Transport and Civil Aviation.

Matt Busby spent the next two months in hospital. Twice he had been given the last rites before finally pulling through, despite his multiple injuries. Months later the manager returned to rebuild his team around the survivors, Gregg, Charlton and Bill Foulkes. He brought in players from other clubs and signed up a brand new talent from Northern Ireland, one George Best. This team went on to beat Leicester City in the 1963 FA Cup Final. Two years later, they won the league, a feat they repeated in 1967.

In tandem with all of these events, the Coleraine man was also making great strides in representing his country, earning twenty-five caps for the Northern Ireland team. Four months after Munich, Gregg sailed, while the rest of his colleagues flew, to Sweden for the 1958 World Cup and was named goalkeeper of the tournament.

Gregg is believed by many to have been the best goalkeeper that Manchester United has ever had, but he incredibly has no silver to show for this. A shoulder injury prevented him from taking part in the 1963 FA Cup victory and further injuries kept him out of additional games, so that he did not qualify for a league championship medal in the 1964-65 and 1966-67 campaigns. He eventually left the club in 1967 when he was transferred to Stoke City, where he spent a year before taking the manager's job at Shrewsbury Town. In 1972 he left Shrewsbury to become manager of Swansea City, a position he held for three years before giving it up to join Crewe Alexandra. Then, in 1978, he was invited back to Manchester United by Dave Sexton to coach goalkeeping. When Sexton left a few years later, so did Gregg. He became assistant at Swindon Town to the manager, Lou Macari, and the team went on to garner the Fourth Division title in 1986. His last role in the sport was as manager of Carlisle United.

He next became an hotelier, buying the Windsor Hotel in Portstewart, which he ran for several years. In 1995 he was awarded an MBE and went on to appear in television documentaries about both Manchester United and the Munich Air Disaster. On the fiftieth anniversary of the crash, Gregg was reunited with Vera Lukic, her daughter Venona, and the baby she was carrying at the time, Zoran, who was by then a journalist. Unfortunately Mr Lukic, who had always wanted to meet the footballer, had recently died.

Harry wrote about his extraordinary experiences in his autobiography, *Harry's Game*.

Henry McCullough (b. 1943)
McCullough was born in the seaside resort of Portstewart and, as soon as he could, embarked on the sort of career that the rest of us can only dream about. He was passionate about music and when he was just sixteen years of age he successfully auditioned to play guitar for the Enniskillen showband, The Skyrockets. He cut his teeth touring around Ireland, performing all the hits of the day, whether they were pop songs or old-time waltzes, while dressed in the suits that were the uniform of the clean cut musicians.

Following a few years of the showband scene McCullough

yearned for something edgier, musically. He enjoyed listening to the likes of The Beatles, The Animals and The Rolling Stones and longed to be a part of the beat music that hit Ireland in the sixties. His dream came true when he was contacted by the Portadown rhythm and blues group, The People, who invited him to play guitar for them. He sold his suits, all twenty-seven of them, and prepared for a stint in Dublin. The People built up quite a following all over Ireland before deciding to travel to London to play at the hip Middle Earth club, supporting Procol Harum and Soft Machine. It was a wise move. The audience included Chas Chandler, who had played bass for The Animals, and was now managing acts like Jimi Hendrix. Chandler was looking for a new act to add to his repertoire and he was immediately impressed by The People, signing them up in 1967. McCullough was now rubbing shoulders with Hendrix and Pink Floyd.

At that stage, wanting to play music was something akin to a vocation. Money was not plentiful; in fact, there was little or none to spare for accommodation. It wasn't unheard of for young musicians, who had travelled to the UK to make it big, to end up sleeping rough for months on end. The People, at least, had a van to sleep in, although its imperfect condition meant they had to park under a railway arch on wet nights. McCullough, in an interview with *The Sunday Times* on 27 April 2006, remembers how he and his colleagues were obliged to frequent religious gatherings in order to enjoy the free sandwiches and tea that were always provided. Their smoking habits, an absolute must for life on the road, were nurtured with second-hand butts that were collected from the ground of Victoria Station. It's hard to imagine a member of Take That or Westlife enduring this sort of lifestyle!

McCullough enjoyed everything initially but cracks appeared when new plans were outlined by the manager. Chandler had the group change their name to Eire Apparent; he wanted them to wear

The distillery at Bushmills.

A session at the Smuggler's Inn, Bushmills.

Mussenden Temple.

Inside Mussenden Temple.

The old Ballywillan Church.

The bridge over the Bann.

The River Bann.

Sunset at Portstewart.

Promenade lights in Portstewart.

The Giant's Causeway.

The Organ pipes, Giant's Causeway.

Coleraine Marina.

outfits similar to those which McCullough thought he had left behind when he'd split from the showband scene. Chandler's influence in the wardrobe department can be seen in his later collaboration with Slade. McCullough decided he had had enough and returned to Ireland where he joined the folk group Sweeney's Men. He was determined to expand his guitar CV as widely as possible by incorporating as many styles as he could; remaining steadfastly loyal to one genre held no attraction for someone who simply loved to play his guitar. Nevertheless he did manage to steer the band towards the innovative sound of folk and rock, and some consider his work at the time to be the finest of his career.

Twelve months later and he was back in London where he was introduced to a singer who was looking for a guitarist. McCullough said yes and found himself whisked off to America for a tour with Joe Cocker and the Grease Band. In 1969 the band took part in that grandmother of festivals, Woodstock, and McCullough can be seen playing away right next to a drenched-in-sweat, high-as-a-flying-kite Cocker who is lost in sound and emptying his lungs out for a fantastic rendition of 'With A Little Help From My Friends'. The guitarist was unimpressed with the gig, describing the historic venue as 'a big muddy field'.

Cocker and his backing band went their separate ways in 1970 and McCullough must have been surprised when he and his Grease Band mates were approached by Tim Rice and Andrew Lloyd Webber who asked them to record the album soundtrack for *Jesus Christ Superstar*. The Grease Band continued playing their hugely popular live concerts for another while. Then, one day, McCullough was introduced to Paul McCartney by Denny Laine, who had played guitar for The Moody Blues. After a three-day audition, Paul invited Henry to join his band with Dennys Laine and Sewell, and, of course, Lynda. This was the original—and some say the best—line-up of Wings. One of their biggest hits was the song 'My Love', from the 1973 album *Red Rose Speedway*. McCullough performs a discreet and understated solo to which the elated Mrs McCartney dances, in a video that can be accessed nowadays on the internet. This guitar solo is still considered today to be one of the very best of its type. When 'My Love' was released as a single it made it to the very top of the US Billboard Top 100.

McCullough contributed to another classic album when Wings were recording next door to Pink Floyd, who were working on the fabulous *Dark Side of The Moon*, at Abbey Road studios. For one song, 'Money', the Floyd wanted some talking voices and Henry was one of a few people, alongside Gerry the doorman, and a couple of technicians, who were asked to say something. His line: 'I was very drunk at the time.'

Henry left Wings in 1973. His clashes with McCartney, whom McCullough felt was too controlling, were becoming more frequent. At one point he told the former Beatle that his guitar bits were 'rubbish'. However, he was not out of work for long, finding himself travelling between America and England to play for some impressive names, including Marianne Faithfull, Ronnie Lane, Donovan, Frankie Miller, Eric Burdon, and the experimental group, Spooky Tooth.

Henry returned to Ireland for a visit in 1984 and almost lost three of his fingers in an accident with a kitchen knife. It would be another three years before he would be able to hold a plectrum again. Like the best accidents the ensuing road to recovery led to some soul searching with a complete reassessment of his life and career. As a result he made two big decisions; he gave up drinking, and decided to stay in Ireland. When he could play his guitar again he joined his buddies, The Fleadh Cowboys, for a weekly Sunday session in the Dublin bar, The Lower Deck. His contribution became a drawing point in itself which pushed McCullough to form his own band and record his own music.

Henry McCullough, a true Irish rock legend, continues to make music and perform to this day.

John Edward McCullough (1832–1885)

John Edward was born in Coleraine, where he lived until he was fifteen years old. He had three sisters: Jane, Mary, and Elizabeth. When he was twelve years of age his beloved mother Mary died, which naturally brought huge changes for the family. His father James was a struggling 'small farmer' and money was always tight. James is described as a distant father with his children. He was also a proud man who battled with financial problems for much of his life. After his wife's death he decided that he couldn't cope with bringing up four children, and perhaps he was encouraged by his relatives, who had settled in Philadelphia, to think about moving abroad. The upshot was that he sent John and Elizabeth over to America to make a new life for themselves. They met up with their cousin, also John, who ran his own chair-making business in Philadelphia and, as soon as they were somewhat settled, their father, along with Jane and Mary, followed them over. Over time the three daughters married and had children. James McCullough worked as a farmer in Philadelphia for the rest of his life. No matter how bad things were for him he refused to take money from his son. He may never have understood or reconciled himself to his son's successful career as an actor. James died in New Jersey in 1878.

John's life was changed utterly on meeting a very fancy customer in his cousin's shop. The fifteen-year-old could read but not write and it seems that he was anxious to learn new things. His cousin's customer was an avid theatre-goer who loved nothing better than talking about Shakespeare and quoting lengthy lines from the Bard's plays, especially *Richard III*, and he discovered an entranced listener in the young boy. He encouraged John to start reading the plays, introducing him to a few theatrical individuals and bringing him to see his first play, *The Apostate*, in Philadelphia's Arch Street Theatre. It proved to be an intoxicating experience for the impressionable boy. He may have felt that this was the reason he had had to pack up and leave everything and everyone he had known in Coleraine. His reaction was swift: he started to read all the plays he could get his hands on and joined his local Boothenian Dramatic Association. The BDA held weekly meetings and gave theatrical performances on the fourth floor of an abandoned warehouse. With the club a new social life was born, and John began to mix with people who shared his passion and dreams to be playing one day to audiences in the most prestigious playhouses. He signed up for elocution lessons and broadened his reading, intent on catching up with his new intellectual friends. For instance, it is said he read and learned by heart most of *Chamber's Encyclopaedia of English Literature*.

All of his effort paid off and he made his professional debut at the Arch Street theatre in 1857. His performance brought him to the attention of one of the big names in the theatre at that time, Edwin Forrest (1806–1872), who immediately adopted him as his protégé and principal supporting actor.

Today's Hollywood community pales in comparison with their acting predecessors. Edwin Forrest, who was of Scottish and German stock, first appeared on the stage in 1820 and made a name for himself with his uncanny ability to portray African-Americans. He would blacken his face and practice his art by mingling on the street with the black community, fooling at least one elderly woman into thinking he was an old friend of hers. One of his greatest performances was in 1826 as Shakespeare's tragic anti-hero Othello. Forrest even got as far as England in 1836, when he performed in *Gladiator*, the play based on the story of the rebel Spartacus, at Drury Lane. He returned to England in 1843 to play Macbeth, but unfortunately his performance was found lacking, resulting in his being promptly booed and hissed at by the English audience. It was also around this time that he fell out with the English actor William Charles Macready (1793–1873). The pair had started off as best friends but then jealousy and rivalry took its toll; Forrest dramatically severed any ties with the English when he went to see Macready act in Edinburgh and loudly hissed at the popular actor from his private box.

Their bitter quarrel was to have far-reaching consequences. As stated, they did start out as friends, with Macready allegedly showing the American actor around London, while Forrest married an English woman whom Macready had introduced him to. Then, for whatever reason, the friendship soured. Their rivalry became infamous, but nobody could have guessed at the outcome. Macready had toured America a couple of times and, in 1849, he arrived at the new Astor Place Opera House in East Eight Street in New York to play Macbeth. It would be his last visit. Anti-English feelings were running high because of the natural disaster that was the potato blight in Ireland, which had led to 1.1 million people dying from starvation—the Great Famine of the late 1840s. The English government had done very little to alleviate the situation, causing a lot of anger inside and outside of Ireland. Macready's only crime was to be English, a former friend of a well-loved American actor, and in New York, surrounded by Irish emigrants, at the worse time possible.

He had already had to battle his way through an earlier performance, acting his way under a barrage of potatoes and smelly liquids which were flung at him on stage; yet he persisted until the end. However, things took a far uglier turn on 10 May when over twenty thousand people gathered on the streets outside the packed theatre. This time, when the poor man made his entrance, he was assailed by insults, curses, and chairs. The chairs were subsequently substituted by paving stones for the second act. It was inevitably suggested to him to give up for the night but he refused, saying, 'The audience has paid for so much, and law compels me to give it; they would have cause for riot, if all were not properly done.'

Meanwhile, activities outside the theatre were—arguably—becoming increasingly more dramatic than anything Shakespeare could have written. The police were obliged to form a protective cordon around the theatre, which allowed them to watch the unruly crowd stone window after window up and down the street. The noise of smashing glass and falling debris only added to the tension and the police, who were hopelessly outnumbered, and with their backs literally up against the wall of the Astor Place House, called in the National Guard from the Seventh Regiment. The Cavalry arrived and were themselves stoned as they marched their way through the crowd to the back of the theatre on Eight Street. They managed to clear this area but when they headed back to the south side of the building the crowd was so large and aggressive that the guards were forced into walking in single file down a very narrow aisle between theatre and mob. The situation was fraught as the guards now felt as outnumbered as the police, and were being continually pelted with rocks. A shocking decision was taken to order the guards to fire their guns at point blank range into the crowd. There were three volleys of shots: the first was over the heads of the crowd and did nothing to quell the storm; the second two were into the crowd—although some of the men refused to fire their weapons at all, while others only continued to fire over the heads of the people. Nevertheless, some did carry out their orders as given and when the crowd at last got the message and began to scatter, there were wounded and dead lying on the ground. This wasn't the end of matters. Fighting continued into the night and more shots were fired by stressed-out police and guards, who killed more rioters. In all, the dead numbered approximately thirty-one citizens with another forty or so injured by bullets, while more than a hundred rioters, police and guards had been wounded by rocks, clubs and all manner of weapons.

Macready was smuggled out of the theatre in disguise and left New York the very next morning. He never returned to the States again. Edwin Forrest, despite his association with the riot, and regardless of a very public divorce later from his English wife, continued to enjoy a successful career. His name lives on today, thanks to his subsequent care of, and generosity towards, his fellow actors. The row with Macready seems to have been a one-off and he used his own personal wealth to shelter actors, especially when the going got tough in 1865, after actor John Wilkes Booth (1838–1865) assassinated Abraham Lincoln (1809–1865), the sixteenth President of the United States. A number of people did not share the President's desire to give black people, including recently emancipated slaves, the right to vote and Booth shot Lincoln as he was enjoying the play, *Our American Cousin*, at Ford's Theatre in Washington DC on 14 April. The story goes that Booth sneaked up behind the President and waited for the funniest line in the play to fire at point-blank range, hoping that the audience's laughter would muffle the sound of the gun. Booth then leapt from the President's box to the stage shouting, 'Sic semper tryannis', which is Latin for 'Thus always to tyrants', the Virginia state motto. There were claims that he also shouted, 'The South is avenged!' He made his escape but a massive manhunt ensued and he was finally cornered and shot dead by Union soldiers in a house in Virginia twelve days later. Incidentally, Booth's brother, Edwin Thomas Booth (1833–1893), is considered by some theatre historians to be the greatest Hamlet of the nineteenth century.

When Edwin Forrest died he left instructions in his will for the construction of the Forrest Home for retired actors in Philadelphia. This establishment prevailed for the next century until it was amalgamated into the much larger Actors Fund facility in New

Jersey, where one of the wings is named the Edwin Forrest Wing. But that was all still in the future.

At some point John McCullough had married a Letitia McClair/McClane and they had two sons, James and William, although only one lived to adulthood. With a family to support he put his all into his acting, which he took very seriously. He was grateful for the attentions of Edwin Forrest and toured with him from 1861 to 1865, allowing himself to be schooled in method and technique by his more experienced mentor. The criticism that his style of acting too closely resembled that of Forrest was voiced on more than one occasion. He is described as being a tall, handsome man, who was physically suited for the role of the hero, which is certainly confirmed by photographs taken of him at the time. When Forrest died in 1872, John was given his starring roles, playing Spartacus in *Gladiator*, as well as the principle parts in productions of *King Lear*, *Antony and Cleopatra*, *Othello*, *Richard III*, *Hamlet* and *Macbeth*.

McCullough also took over managerial duties of San Francisco's California Theatre with fellow actor, Lawrence Barrett (1838–1891), and continued to do so when Barrett left in 1870. However, he was forced to give up seven years later and returned to the stage full-time, having found himself in severe financial difficulties. He spent the rest of his life touring in his favourite roles. In April 1881 he played at London's Drury Lane and received a better reception than Edwin Forrest had years before, although the critics gave him somewhat mixed reviews. For instance, the *Standard* wrote, 'Mr McCullough was warmly applauded by a very cordial house. His shortcomings as an artist are the absence of real passion and the inaudibility of the lower tones of his voice, but there were some striking moments in his interpretation.' Meanwhile, the *Telegraph* shared the opinion of McCullough's audience: 'He came, was seen and conquered.'

The next two years passed happily enough. McCullough was a popular man, whose qualities included integrity and kindness. He was at the pinnacle of his career, and America's elite flocked to see him perform. Then, one night, in 1883, it looked as if he had stumbled over his lines. He was playing Spartacus, a role he was thoroughly familiar with. A few nights later the audience hissed and laughed at him because they thought he was drunk. His co-star and friend, Joseph Haworth, recognised that something was wrong and began to deliver the lead's speeches as well as his own, prompting McCullough to tell him morosely, mid-performance, 'You're saying my words', which cracked the audience up. But he wasn't drunk; he was actually experiencing the early stages of general paresis, a disorder which affects the brain and central nervous system. His last stage appearance was in Chicago in 1884. By now his behaviour was so erratic that he was taken into the Bloomingdale Asylum in the summer of 1885. Joseph Haworth, in an essay about his friend written some years after his death, describes how McCullough became obsessed with study and books, and during a visit would unknowingly repeat the same passage from a play, over and over again, asking Haworth for a comment. His relationship with his wife had declined over the years and they no longer lived together. However, they remained on the best of terms. On some of his visits to her, his illness caused him to state that he had to be leaving immediately for an important appointment, although no such appointment actually existed. A short time later he lost the power of speech, a bitter affliction for one whose main love in life was the spoken word. A few months after his admittance, McCullough was released from the asylum at the request of his wife who, despite suffering from cancer, nursed him until his death that same year. She was to die soon after him.

This was a sad end for a great talent and a good man, but the story doesn't finish there. McCullough's ghost was reportedly seen in various parts of the National Theatre in Washington DC, making sure that everything was in order before the curtain went up before a performance, checking the props and the scenery, and generally roaming around. Some described him as being dressed as Hamlet, which was the first role he had ever performed in the Washington theatre, while others saw him dressed in his Spartacus costume. One of the actors, who had known McCullough, saw his ghost sitting in an orchestra chair, right beside the gas footlights, calmly watching the play as if it were a normal member of the audience. Over the years there were many sightings reported by doormen, night watchmen, actors and stagehands, who saw him backstage, in dressing rooms, on staircases and, not surprisingly, on stage when there was nobody about.

In 1896, eleven years after his death, the *Washington Post*, in their 4 October edition, printed a story about the actor Frederic Bond, who had been a close friend of McCullough. It was late one night and Bond was working on his lines for the following day's rehearsal. As far as he was concerned he was the only one left in the theatre, apart from the night watchman. He was seated at a table at the front of the stage, reading his lines aloud by gaslight when he heard a strange noise. Slightly distracted by his work he briefly looked to the wings and into the dark auditorium but there was nobody there, so he resumed his reading. Almost immediately another noise jolted him from his script and he thought that someone had just walked behind the stage curtains. Maybe it was the night watchman, or a fellow actor playing a trick on him. Suddenly, the hairs on the back of his neck stood up in salute and he felt that something out of the ordinary was taking place. Panic gripped him and he went to call out when someone walked or glided on to the stage, stopping just in front of him. Frederic recognised his old friend and greeted him in bewilderment, 'John McCullough! John!' Alas, the apparition turned away from him and walked solemnly to the wings before disappearing. Before Frederic could collect his thoughts, a second figure appeared on stage. Just recently the death had occurred of a young stagehand, Eddie Specht, who had yearned to be an actor. Specht had idolised McCullough and was known to imitate the Coleraine man's acting on the empty stage. It was the transparent shadow of Eddie who appeared before Frederic now, following McCullough's spirit to the wings, before disappearing at the exact spot that John had. More sightings of the pair followed, with Eddie always silently following McCullough around the theatre. These apparitions persisted well into the twentieth century.

The story became so big that, in the 1930s, the Washington police talked about digging up the floor beneath the theatre. Fanciful conjecture and theatrical lore by this time had John McCullough buried in a cellar beneath the stage after having been murdered by a fellow actor. When the theatre was built in 1835 it sat upon the Tiber Creek, whose water could be heard flowing in the auditorium during very quiet scenes or after a heavy rainfall. The cast of the plays performed there would often wash their costumes in the clean running water. It wasn't until the 1950s that the creek was enclosed in a storm sewer. The story went that McCullough had apparently got into an argument with a young colleague who was a member of the same touring company as they both did their laundry beneath the stage. One version has the two men fighting over an actress from the company, while another has them arguing over a coveted role. After much shouting by the two, shots were heard and John McCullough was dead. Conspiracy ensued when the company contrived to keep the whole business as quiet as possible, hastily burying the esteemed actor in a makeshift grave that was later cemented over. The Washington police proposed digging up the body to investigate the rumoured murder but the management of the theatre encouraged them to forget about it.

Over fifty years later, in 1982, the theatre underwent a massive refurbishment, during which a rusted old pistol, dating from approximately 1850, was discovered in the dirt beneath the stage and handed over to the Smithsonian Institute. Whether this nugget of information reveals anything about why McCullough's apparition had been reported in the vicinity over the years is debatable.

James Nesbitt (b.1965)

Nesbitt was not born in Coleraine but let's not hold that against him. When he was eleven years old his family moved to Blagh, near Coleraine, where he attended the Academical Institution and began his acting career, thanks to a teacher's encouragement, at the Riverside Theatre. He made his stage debut at thirteen years of age, playing the Artful Dodger in a production of *Oliver!* More roles were to follow; yet Nesbitt decided that he wanted to be a teacher like his father and sisters. Accordingly, he registered at the University of Ulster in Jordanstown, but his studies suffered due to more pleasant distractions like girls and football. It was his father who suggested that he move to England to enrol at the Central School of Speech and Drama, and so it began.

Almost as soon as he graduated from drama school in 1987, he got himself an agent and a small part in a BBC film, earning a whopping £500 for just two days work. After that he was back on stage, followed by a tour of *Hamlet*, a production in which he had three roles. He had a critical breakthrough with the role of Fintan O'Donnell in *Hear My Song*, the 1992 film loosely based on the life of Irish tenor, Josef Locke (1917-1999), which starred Ned Beatty, Adrian Dunbar and Tara Fitzgerald. The film was nominated for Best Original Screenplay at the 1993 BAFTA Awards, and more importantly, led to Nesbitt being cast in 1996 in the one-off romantic comedy *Cold Feet*. The director, Declan Lowney, was a friend but Nesbitt had to audition for the role, which had not originally been written for an Irish man. When the programme was broadcast a year later, it won the Golden Rose of Montreux, which led to a commission for a further six episodes. It was to become one of the most popular series on British television.

The Golden Rose of Montreux is a highly prestigious television award that was established in Switzerland, back in 1961. It is presented each spring at the Festival Rose d'Or and concentrates solely on entertainment programmes. Usually forty countries are represented at Montreux and, apart from presenting awards, the festival also acts as a trade fair, in that the different nations get to showcase their best television shows in the hope that they will be bought by foreign broadcast companies. The first British winner in 1961 was *The Black and White Minstrel Show*, while others to have carried home the trophy include *Mr Bean*, *Pop Idol* and *Little Britain*.

In 1996 Nesbitt appeared in one episode of the BBC Northern Ireland series *Ballykissangel*, playing Dervla Kirwin's boyfriend, Leo McGarvey. He returned to the series two years later to appear in another five episodes. That same year, he gained international attention for his portrayal of 'Pig' Finn in the film *Waking Ned*, starring alongside David Kelly and Ian Bannen. The film was about an elderly lottery winner who dies of shock, leading his village neighbours to collaborate in 'keeping him alive' so that they can claim his winnings instead. *Ned* did especially well in America, earning the actors involved a nomination in 1999 for the Screen Actors' Guild Award for Outstanding Performance by a Cast in a Theatrical Motion Picture. In fact, the film received nine different nominations in a variety of festivals around the world, winning seven of them.

Meanwhile *Cold Feet* continued to play to rave reviews and brought Nesbitt three British Comedy Awards nominations. He won the gong for Best TV Comedy Actor in 2000, and this was followed by a National Television Award for Most Popular Comedy Actor in 2003.

More projects followed in film and television but perhaps one of the most important, and controversial, roles was that of the Derry politician, Ivan Cooper, in the 2001 factual drama *Bloody Sunday*, directed by Paul Greengrass. Cooper, who was born into a Protestant working-class family in Killaloo, County Londonderry, was one of the major figures of the 1960s Civil Rights' Movement, and a founder of the Social Democratic and Labour Party (SDLP). On 30 January 1972 he led a peaceful—but illegal—march to protest against internment which ended in tragedy when the marchers were fired upon by soldiers of the Parachute Regiment. Unionists had grave concerns about the drama, while actual threats were made on Nesbitt's life. However, he must have been pleased with the positive reaction to his work; he won Best Actor at the British Independent Film Awards, as well as at the Stockholm Film Festival. Suddenly he was being perceived in a brand new light, as a serious dramatic actor.

The novelist, Colin Bateman, who is a close friend of Nesbitt, created the character of smooth-talking undercover police officer DS Tommy Murphy in his book *Murphy's Law*. When Nesbitt played Murphy in the televised version, it was the start of something big. *Murphy's Law* returned to the BBC for a full series in 2003, and since then there have been five series in all, which have become progressively more dramatic and dark.

In 2007 Nesbitt played Pontius Pilate in *The Passion*, a BBC/HBO production, after a bit of prompting from his agent. He had other commitments and felt he wouldn't be able to take the job. It was only after his agent insisted that he read the script one more time that he thought again about the piece and agreed to participate. Nesbitt used his own accent and decided to play a humane and amiable Pilate, one that the viewer could relate to.

There are plenty of other projects too numerous to mention here, including the Yellow Pages television advertisements, and the acclaimed thriller, *Jekyll*, but acting is not the only thing in Jimmy Nesbitt's life. He has been a UNICEF ambassador since 2005, a role which has brought him face to face with HIV and Aids sufferers, as well as former child soldiers in Africa. He is also a patron of both WAVE, the charity which was set up to help those who have been traumatised by the Troubles, and Action Cancer.

Football is a serious passion. Nesbitt is a huge Coleraine FC and Manchester United fan. When the Coleraine team were in severe financial difficulties in 2003, the actor made a personal donation to get them back on track. That same year the University of Ulster awarded him an honorary Doctorate of Letters for his contribution to drama.

Robert 'Bertie' Peacock (1928-2004)

Peacock was born in Coleraine on 29 September. Not surprisingly his football career began with his local club, Coleraine FC, and it began in grand style, on a particularly good day, when the team trounced Ballymena United 4–1 in the Connor Cup. The talented eighteen-year-old played a few more matches for his home town before moving on to play for the Belfast club, Glentoran, in 1947. He spent two years here, and scored the only goal of the 1949 Irish Cup Final, against Barney Cannon's Derry City squad. He then got his big break, being signed up for the Glasgow giants, Celtic, a club he would represent 450 times. His debut match as a 'bhoy', at inside left, took place in a Scottish League Cup match against Aberdeen which ended in a draw.

His time at Celtic brought him legendary status. He was part of the youngest ever Celtic team to win the Scottish Cup. The squad won the League and Cup double in 1954. Two years later he was on the first ever Celtic team to win the League Cup; they beat

Partick Thistle 3-0 in a replay. One can safely assume that 1957 was important for the Coleraine man as this was the year in which he captained the Celtic team that smashed Rangers in the League Cup final with the unbelievable result of seven goals to one.

Things got even better in 1958 when Peacock played for his country in the World Cup. Nobody would have guessed that Northern Ireland would reach the Quarter Final in Sweden. Peacock's dynamite performance on the field endeared him to the Swedish media who dubbed him 'The Little Black Ant' because he was everywhere, as busy as an ant on the pitch against the likes of Czechoslovakia (twice), Argentina and West Germany. He was further applauded for his goal, albeit disallowed, in the play-off match against Czechoslovakia, as he was badly injured at the time.

He went on to represent his country thirty-one times, scoring two goals. In all, he scored fifty goals in 453 games. When he left Celtic in 1961 he was offered management positions with both Morton and Blackpool but he preferred instead to return home to play for and manage his old club at The Showgrounds. He also managed Northern Ireland, from 1962 to 1967, succeeding Peter Doherty, and giving two other talented young players their debut in 1964, against Wales: George Best and Pat Jennings.

Under his supervision Coleraine won all the domestic trophies and two Blaxnit All-Ireland Cups in 1969 and 1970. In 1970 there was tremendous excitement when Coleraine eliminated Kilmarnock in the Fairs Cup after beating them 3–2 in Scotland. Two years later they beat Portadown in the Irish Cup Final and then, in 1974, Peacock took Coleraine to their first ever Irish League Championship. He stepped down officially as manager after this achievement but in reality he continued to play a huge role in the club and was always available as advisor and supporter. In 1982 he was asked by Billy Bingham to be 'Chief Assessor' for

Northern Ireland's World Cup campaign, when they knocked out the hosts Spain in Valencia.

He also set up the Milk Cup with Jim Weir and Victor Leonard. This youth football competition, which is held in Coleraine, started out with just sixteen teams in 1982 and has gone from strength to strength since. Four years later Peacock was awarded the MBE for his services to football. He died, following a short illness, in 2004.

A statue to celebrate the footballer and manager was commissioned in 2006. Following a storm of fundraising events the statue of Peacock in his football kit, by artist Ross Wilson, was unveiled in 2007 by Pat Jennings at the opening of the twenty-fifth Milk Cup.

Oliver Pollock (1737–1823)

Pollock was born in Coleraine. In 1760, when he was twenty-three years of age, he and his father emigrated to the United States where they settled down in Cumberland County, Pennsylvania. Within two years Pollock had embarked on a lucrative business career which required him to move to Havana, Cuba. Here he traded from port to port with the Spaniards in the West Indies and cleverly befriended the Governor-General Don Alejandro O'Reilly. It was a sound friendship that would last a lifetime. When O'Reilly was made Governor of Louisiana by the King of Spain, Pollock moved his business to New Orleans where he was granted free trade by the Louisiana officials thanks to his good standing with their new governor. In 1765 (some accounts name 1770 as the year of his nuptials) Pollock married Miss Margaret O'Brien, from the prominent and wealthy O'Brien family. They went on to have eight children before her death in 1799.

Alejandro (originally Alexander) O'Reilly (1722–1794) was born in Dublin, which he then left when old enough to find employment in foreign Catholic armies. He was one of thousands of young Irish men and women who chose to leave home in the sixteenth, seventeenth and eighteenth centuries in the face of English oppression, and who are collectively known today as the Wild Geese. Spain was an early refuge for these emigrants, as was France and Austria in the eighteenth century. True to form, O'Reilly became a colonel in the Austrian army. In 1762 he took part in Spain's invasion of Portugal and switched his allegiance, becoming a brigadier general in the Spanish army. The following year he accompanied the new Spanish governor, the Count of Ricla, to Havana, a city that had been recently won back from British forces in the latter days of the Seven Years War.

Food was scarce in New Orleans in 1769, allowing Pollock to make a noble and generous gesture. Some French Creoles had rebelled against the Spanish authorities, expelling Spain's first governor, Antonio de Ulloa, from the colony. O'Reilly's three thousand troops had arrived, immediately doubling the population, and provisions that had been specially ordered had failed to arrive. What did turn up, however, was a ship of flour belonging to Pollock. He had bought the ship in Baltimore, Maryland, and had it loaded with flour which was selling for approximately $30 a barrel, a fairly respectable sum at the time. When he heard about the missing provisions Pollock went straight to O'Reilly and told him that he could have his flour and the Governor could set the price. O'Reilly demurred so Pollock set the price, cutting his potential profit in half, by insisting on selling his barrels at just $15 each. It would not be forgotten; when O'Reilly informed the Spanish monarch about the discount the King replied that Pollock would always enjoy a prosperous business in that part of the world; he would personally make sure of it.

By now Pollock was a hugely successful businessman and plantation owner, and it appears that he was as popular as he was rich. His popularity might have stemmed from the fact that he was obviously a man of principle who believed in loyalty to his chosen cause. For instance, in 1775, with the declaration of war between Britain and the American colonies, Pollock nailed his colours to the mast of the American side and it seemed that all his experiences and achievements to date had been for just such an occasion.

The American Revolutionary War was the indirect fallout from the British victory in the battle against the royal French forces and their various American Indian allies, during the Seven Years War (1754–1763). Britain now ruled all of New France, east of the Mississippi River, including Spanish Florida; France was obliged to reimburse Spain, her ally, for losing Florida by making a present of French Louisiana, which was west of the Mississippi. Once the French military threat had been soundly quelled the British wanted thanks from their American colonists, reasoning that this gratitude should come in the shape of hard currency. Colonists were expected to make substantial contributions towards the costs of being kept within the Empire and, to this end, the British brought in several new taxes along with other equally unpopular laws. The irony was that the angry colonists felt their rights as Englishmen had been violated since they lacked any personal representatives in the English parliament. In 1772 Patriot groups began to set up committees of correspondence, forerunners of the Provincial Congress which would be established in the majority of the colonies. In time these committees replaced British 'law and order', coming together under the banner of the Continental Congress. A cauldron of resentment and ill-feeling finally boiled over in 1775 with the outbreak of fighting between the British Empire and her Americans colonists. The following year a Declaration of Independence was issued by representatives of the thirteen colonies, and the United States of America was born.

Spain played a pivotal role during this war, coming firmly down on the side of the colonies. She protected the American southern coastline from the British and also supplied Patrick Henry (1736–1799), the Governor of Virginia, and future president George Washington (1732–1799), with war essentials, such as guns, ammunition and food. However, it was Coleraine man Oliver Pollock who set up the whole operation, using his own money to fund the American defence and negotiating with the Spanish to have supplies sent to the northwest, to the forces under the command of George Rogers Clark.

George Rogers Clark (1752–1818) was a soldier from Albemarle County, Virginia, who became an important general during the Revolutionary War. He earned his name 'Conqueror of the Northwest' after capturing the posts Kasaskia (1778), a village in Randolph County, Illinois, and Vincennes (1779), the oldest town in Indiana; two great blows to the British. When the Treaty of Paris was signed on 3 September 1783, signalling the end of conflict between Britain and the United States, the British handed over the entire Northwest Territory, thus making Clark a hero in this part of the world. This proved to be Clark's greatest moment, which was never to be repeated. All his acts of glory were completed by the time he reached the age of thirty and the rest of his life was mostly consumed by battles of a different kind, against alcoholism and poverty. During the war it had been necessary for him to borrow huge sums of money in order to run his army and apparently all the expenditure records were filed in Richmond, Virginia, where they were burnt to ash during an attack in 1781. Consequently, when Clark's creditors came calling, he had no means of being properly reimbursed by his home county.

On 12 June 1777 Pollock was given a unique opportunity when he was chosen by the Secret Committee of the United States, which was under the Continental Congress, and included the likes of future president, Benjamin Franklin, Robert Morris and Charles

Lee, to be Commercial Agent of the United States in New Orleans; in other words, he would now represent the colonies in the city. It was a position of the utmost importance, especially during wartime. Morris, a wealthy merchant, became known as a Financier of the American Revolution and like Pollock ended up in the debtors' prison after the war. He was also one of the signatories to the Declaration of Independence and the new American constitution. Lee, from Cheshire, England, was a British soldier turned Virginia planter. He was a general of the Continental Army during the war and had a spectacular fall from grace owing to his jealousy and bitterness towards the infinitely more popular George Washington.

Meanwhile Don Bernardo de Gálvez (1746–1786), previously Colonel of the Regiment of Louisiana, had been made Governor of Louisiana on 1 February 1777. Gálvez's father was Viceroy of Mexico while his uncle was the Spanish Secretary of State. He and Pollock became firm friends, with Pollock being described at the time as the only man—and the only British merchant!—that Gálvez would, or could, confide in. For the next two years, Pollock organised a secret smuggling operation between the Spanish and the Americans. Gálvez was his partner-in-crime who did his best to pretend he was neutral in front of the British. Part of his job as Governor was to prevent illegal smuggling from taking place, so an American ship would be loaded down with goods and given a time and position to approach the American shore, whereupon it would be melodramatically 'caught' by the Governor's men and its crew would be 'arrested' and warned that they were in 'big trouble', as far the British were concerned. Naturally it was all a hoax and, for the most part, it worked. The British were happy with Gálvez's efforts; that is until he had British ships—properly—arrested for the exact same crime. Then Spain spoiled Gálvez's front by declaring war on Britain on 21 June 1779 and entering into a treaty with France, but the Governor did his best to behave as if he was ignorant of his new status, as an enemy of Britain. He refrained from announcing to his men that they were now at war with Britain, two months after the fact was made known to him. Instead his focus was on securing the Mississippi River. Just before he could launch his attack a fierce hurricane throttled New Orleans, causing severe damage to several of his ships and leaving the city open to attack. Some weeks were needed for repairs to the city and her defences and, eventually, on 27 August, Gálvez set out on foot with 667 men for Fort Manchac while a small number of ships sailed up the Mississippi. He was joined by his friend, and official Agent of Virginia and the Continental Congress, Oliver Pollock, who served as his aide. Almost two weeks later, on 6 September, when he had Fort Manchac in his sights, Gálvez finally informed his men that they were actually at war with Britain and, accordingly, would be taking the British-held fort by force, or whatever means possible.

The next day the Governor's small army ventured to take Fort Bute, and as it turned out, they had an easy time of it because the British had began to suspect that Gálvez was trouble and had pre-empted an attack by moving their main force north to Baton Rouge, an important stronghold. Undaunted, Gálvez led his men in pursuit. When they reached the fort he took a few days to plan the next move. On 20 September he gave orders for a battery to be erected and went on the offensive, commencing fire on the British, keeping their attention firmly on this section of his army, while leaving a handful of his men free to quickly erect a second battery in range of the fort. So it was that, on 21 September, the fort was attacked and Gálvez's men were victorious. They took Baton Rouge, and furthermore, in order that the British be allowed to surrender, the fort at Panmure was also handed over, albeit by a bewildered British commander who hadn't even known that the

Spanish were in the area. It fell to the Spanish captain, Juan Delavillebeuvre, to update him on the recent events.

It was through Gálvez that Oliver Pollock borrowed $70,000 which he used to fund the campaign of George Rogers Clark in the Northwest Territory and strengthen the defence of the frontier. It would seem that the backers of the revolution paid unfairly for their economic initiative in the aftermath of the war. In 1783 Pollock was still in Havana, where he was made United States Agent, and a year later, he was imprisoned for the debt he had incurred as a result of his involvement with the war, which was something in the region of $150,000. When Oliver was released on parole in 1785, he returned to Cumberland County in Pennsylvania. There he bumped into Robert Morris who, being naturally sympathetic to the situation, scraped together some money to keep the debt collectors temporarily from Oliver's door. Another six years would pass before Congress discharged Pollock's debt, although he was never paid for his services to the country. And he wasn't the only one to suffer in this way. Robert Morris, who had also financed the American forces, endured hard monetary times as a result, and in 1798 was thrown into prison for three years, after having become involved in a bad land speculation deal. One of his colleagues during the war was a Polish Jew called Haym Salomon (1740–1785). Salomon had proven his loyalty to the new America when he was imprisoned by the British in New York for helping the revolutionaries, and was sentenced to death. However, he managed to escape to Philadelphia instead where he set up a successful brokerage business. From there he helped Morris to obtain loans from France, as well as making available his own personal fortune to the new government. By the time the war was over Salomon's money was gone and, as with others like him, he never received a cent for his efforts. His wife was pregnant with their fourth child, and had already three children under the age of seven, when the impoverished Salomon died from tuberculosis.

The Revolutionary War had been a costly one with the national debt falling mainly into three categories: $11 million was owed to foreigners, particularly to France; and there were two lots of debt, of approximately $24 million each, owed by the national and state governments to Americans and individuals, such as Morris, Salomon and Pollock, who had sold or bought food, horses and ammunition for the revolutionary forces. The rest of the debt was down to the promissory notes that were issued to soldiers, merchants and farmers throughout the war years, with the plan that the notes would be redeemed by the new government which was still to be put in place. Congress agreed that the power and authority of the new government would deal with the foreign debt. Then, in 1790, Congress decided, on the suggestion of the first Secretary of the Treasury, to combine all of the different debts into a grand total of $80 million.

Despite his continuing poverty Oliver was nominated for Congress in 1797, 1804 and 1806, but he was never successful beyond his home county, even though he constantly took the popular vote. In 1800 he suffered another period behind bars when he ended up in Philadelphia's debtors' prison, but ultimately, he was luckier than Haym Salomon. A widower since 1799 he remarried, in 1805, to a Winifred Deady; they had no children. Maybe it was around this time that he managed to acquire some property again and, in 1815 (or 1819, depending on the accuracy of the record), he retired to Mississippi, where he lived until his death in 1823.

Apart from his important role in the success of the American forces during the war Oliver Pollock left his mark on something else: something as enduring as American independence; something that could even be described as being iconic of that independence.

It is generally believed that Pollock was the creator of the dollar sign. As a successful trader and plantation owner he did a lot of business with the Spanish outpost in New Orleans, where he would naturally use their currency, the peso. He drew an abbreviation for the coinage which, in his hand-writing, looked for all the world like a backward 'p' and 's'. Just before 1775 it was obvious that a decision needed to be made about the national monetary system and Congress felt that it would make sense to use the most commonly circulated coins at the time, which were Spanish coins. Up to that point English pounds were the tool of the American businessman, and, in the 1770s, the search began for an alternative. Lo and behold the 'Spanish Milled Dollar' made its entry, and after a short while, was affectionately known as just plain old 'dollar'. Pollock's '$' was constantly dotted about the records and receipts that he sent to Congressman Robert Morris, who obviously got used to it. In fact, Morris was the first government official to approve of the symbol. About twenty years later, in 1797, the dollar sign was established as a recognisable part of American identity when it appeared in a book by Chauncey Lee.

Another story concerns Pollock in his role as plantation and slave owner. Of course, slavery was perfectly legal in the United States from 1654 to 1865. In 1794 Pollock and his family were living on a large estate, called the James Silver Estate, and he bought a young slave girl by the name of Chloe. Thanks to a law passed in 1780, Pennsylvania slave owners were now required to register the births of slave babies, which is why we know that Chloe was born in December 1782. There is no mother or father mentioned; baby Chloe is registered by William Kelso, who ran a busy inn and a ferry service. He owned two hundred acres, six cows, four horses and two male Negro slaves. When she was eleven years old Chloe was handed over to a slave dealer who sold her on two weeks later to a landowner. He also sold her on and, over the next four months, she was sold a total of five times, until eventually she was bought by Oliver Pollock. She lived in his house for the next two years before being sold yet again, this time to Arthur Carothers, who was to be her last master. Chloe was the first slave that Carothers had ever owned and no doubt she was purchased at his wife's insistence to help her manage a busy house with six children.

There are no details about what type of person Chloe was. However, in light of the amount of times she was sold in her short life, it can be assumed that hers was not the easiest of childhoods, which may or may not account for her murdering two of the Carothers children: four-year-old Lucetta and six-year-old Polly. Both were drowned by the slave girl in the creek beside their farm. At the subsequent trial, it emerged that Mrs Carothers would routinely beat Chloe every day whether she had done something wrong or not, and the children had also been encouraged to monitor their slave's behaviour and report back to their parents about her. In her confession Chloe explained that she loved the children, but had reached breaking point due to the brutal treatment meted out by her mistress. She also remarked that Pollock had been the only master that she had liked and respected, referring to her time in his charge as the happiest in her life. He had taken the time to teach her something about religious instruction and the rudimentary basics of life.

Nevertheless, Chloe was sentenced to hang. Four objections were immediately raised in the courtroom against the death penalty, citing the fact that Chloe's confession had been beaten from her, and that Mrs Carothers had been the only witness questioned in court about the whole affair, but it was all in vain. On Saturday, 18 July 1801, at 12am, Chloe was hanged on a temporary gallows.

Edward Sheil (1834–1869)

Sheil was born in Coleraine, but moved to Cork to enrol at the School of Art, where he developed and honed his talent until he was ready to exhibit his work in 1855 to favourable reviews at the Royal Hibernian Academy in Dublin. Two years later he was appointed Second Master at the School of Art under the Head Master David Wilkie Rainbach, whose godfather and former teacher was the Scottish artist, David Wilkie.

Sir David Wilkie (1785-1841) made his name painting historical and religious subjects. He also painted the odd portrait, including a rather flattering one of King George IV that had previously caused him some difficulty, when his realist side fought an internal battle with his aesthetic side. In 1822 King George made an official visit to Scotland, the first by a reigning monarch since 1650, and David was given the honour of painting him to celebrate and commemorate the special occasion. The King was not the most attractive of beings and David worried about insulting him with an honest portrait. In fact, the artist deliberated for quite a while over how exactly he was going to approach the commission. In the end he gave into creativity, and thereby, flattery. He 'slimmed' the podgy King down, and used subtle colours to undermine the brightness of George's flamboyant red tartan which, sadly, did not compliment its wearer. Furthermore he 'neglected' to paint the shocking pink tights that the King wore under his scarlet kilt to hide his 'muscular' legs. It was a wise move and, in 1836, the artist received a knighthood from King George, who became a lifelong fan.

Sheil taught mechanical drawing and proved to be a popular teacher in the school, which might have been one of the reasons why, on Wilkie's retirement in 1859, he was appointed Head Master. Unfortunately, he was forced to resign from the position after only twelve months because of his fragile health. Pupils and staff were disappointed to see him leave and were presumably even more dismayed when his successor, Thomas Frederick Collier, who specialised in twilight and moonlit scenes, spent most of his time in thrall of alcoholic rather than aesthetic inspiration. His short career as Head Master ended one morning when pupils arrived to find him surrounded by the debris of an alcohol-fuelled rage, during which he had smashed numerous plaster casts. A short while later he left Cork, his wife and his children.

Meanwhile Sheil decided to travel to the warmer climate of Rome in a bid to improve his health and continue his own study of art. Apart from the fact that he had to give up a job he'd enjoyed, 1860 was not a bad year for him as four of his paintings were put on display at the RHA. He now had more time to concentrate on painting.

A particularly industrious artist, he returned to Cork in 1861, along with his family, and set up a studio at 4 Great George's Street in the city. Here he began working on four paintings, 'The Labourer's Sunday Morning', 'Blind Mary', 'The Epiphany' and 'The Man of Sorrows'. There was a very complimentary review of the works in the *Cork Examiner* when they were exhibited in the RHA. It should be noted, however, that Edward's brother, George, who was described as being 'devoted' to his talented sibling, was a journalist with said paper, which probably did no harm to the artist when it came to both coverage and reviews.

Sheil's paintings usually depict contented family life, religious subjects, romance and emigration. His roles as husband and father must have been ultimately fulfilling as happy families crop up time and time again in his work. For instance, one of his best known paintings, 'Home After Work' (1863) centres on a doting but worn-out father, who, at the end of a long day and, having finished his dinner, is carefully taking his baby in his arms. His wife's gaze is filled with love as she regards her little family. The dining room looks warm and cosy; this isn't a materially rich family but they are certainly rich in the things that matter. Some critics think that the artist is referring to the Holy Family in this piece, as Sheil was known to be a religious man. When the painting went on display at the RHA it was snapped up by the Earl of Carlisle, Lord Lieutenant of Ireland.

Edward continued to paint throughout the 1860s. In 1861 he was elected as an Associate Member of RHA. Four years later he moved his family to Queenstown (Cobh), in Cork harbour, which was a well-known health resort at the time, and where he set up another studio on the beach. Once again he received a visit from the *Cork Examiner*, whose writer was enraptured by the three paintings that were in progress.

Sheil was influenced by his surroundings and this showed in such work as 'The Emigrant', 'Left Behind – Ireland 1868', and 'A Long Last Look Towards Home'. Queenstown was where hundreds of Cork people boarded the emigrant ships bound for a new life in America. It was less than twenty years since the catastrophe of the Great Famine and the effects were still being felt in the large numbers of people continuing to leave Ireland. In describing 'Left Behind', the *Examiner* journalist applauded Sheil for showcasing great emotional power in his illustration of 'the daily Irish tragedy'. This picture went on display at the RHA in 1868.

Sheil moved his family one more time, this time back into Cork, where he set up what was to be his last studio, at 10 Granville Place. It must have been a very difficult time for his family as his health deteriorated considerably while few of his paintings sold. Sheil finally passed away as a consequence of tuberculosis, or 'consumption', on 11 March 1869, in the house of his good friend, fellow painter, poet and patriot, Denny Lane. Within two years of his death his pictures were sought after by all manner of collectors, a trend which persists today.

Hugh Thomson (1860-1920)

Thomson was born in Coleraine, attending the Model School, before heading to Belfast, where, as a teenager, he got a job with the linen merchants, Gibbon & Sons, on the Strand Road. When his mother Catherine Andrews died, his father, who was a tea merchant, married Kilrea woman, Maria Lennox.

It is probably safe to assume that Thomson discovered his love for drawing at an early age and, in between his hours at Gibbon & Sons, he worked on developing his talent. Of course, he had taken a few art classes at school but he was largely self-taught. His destiny unfolded when he was recommended to Marcus Ward, owner of the eponymous award-winning stationery, colour-printing and publishing business. On seeing the impressive portfolio which Hugh had built up in his spare time, this prestigious Belfast publishing company—which had an international reputation—offered him an apprenticeship in its art department. Head designer John Vinycomb took the budding artist under his wing and, over the next six years, tutored him in the complexities of illustration.

Vinycomb (1833–1928) had left his home town of Newcastle-upon-Tyne and arrived in Belfast in 1855, where he established himself both as an authority on heraldry and as a much sought after designer of bookplates. He was a sociable man who integrated very well into the city's cultural scene, becoming president of the Belfast Arts Society, the Belfast Naturalists Field Club, and the Ulster Arts Club. He made a huge impression on his young student, as is very much in evidence in Thomson's later work, particularly in his ability to capture the minute detail in both stationary objects and the expressions of character. In 1883, the twenty-three-year-old Thomson moved to London to join *The English Illustrated Magazine*, published by Macmillan. It was an exciting time to be in the publishing business; the Victorian Age had inspired a new fascination with society which prompted a surge of interest in the arts. People were reading more and thinking more about the world and its inhabitants. Revolutions in the printing process meant that books were cheaper and more widely available than ever before, and publications also looked more accessible, more colourful, more appealing. Artwork could now be reproduced within the pages of a novel to complement the story; the age of the illustrator was upon us.

Thomson's drawings for the Macmillan magazine caused a flurry of excitement within the book world and soon the Coleraine illustrator was working freelance, such was the volume of work that was offered to him. In 1890 Macmillan had him illustrate Oliver Goldsmith's novel, *The Vicar of Wakefield*. The project was a runaway success, which resulted in him being asked to illustrate two more novels the following year: Elizabeth Gaskell's *Cranford*, and *Our Village* by Mary Russell Mitford. Thomson's line drawings for these books were much loved for their delicacy and humour, and were also imbued with nostalgia, evoking the 'good old days' before the ambiguities of the Industrial Revolution.

The Gaskell novel certainly proved to be a defining moment for its illustrator, and his style was afterwards frequently referred to as the 'Cranford School' and garnered him many admirers among the young artists then studying the profession. Another publisher, George Allen, asked Thomson to illustrate a very pretty edition of Jane Austen's *Pride and Prejudice*, resulting in Macmillan contracting him again to illustrate the other five Austen novels in 1896 and 1897. The Austen-Thomson publications were a perfect marriage of styles, and the books are still lauded today for Thomson's portrayal of the world famous characters, with his drawings brimming with personality and drama.

Huge Thomson was now one of the top three Victorian illustrators and he proceeded to contribute to many other works, including books by J M Barrie, Charles Dickens, George Eliot, Nathaniel Hawthorne, William Shakespeare and Richard Brinsley

Sheridan. His drawings and books are now collectors' items, with prices varying from the hundreds to the thousands.

In 2003 Coleraine Borough Council were offered the chance to buy over eight hundred pieces of Thomson's work from a Belfast bookseller, who had acquired the collection from a nephew of the illustrator over thirty years previously. The 540 watercolours, 168 books and magazine illustrations, including original drawings for *Emma* by Jane Austen and William Thackeray's *Vanity Fair*, are now on display in the Coleraine Museum.

Charles Williams (1838-1904)

was born in Coleraine. He attended a school in Cross Lane which was run by an American clergyman, and strict disciplinarian, the Reverend Higginson, who wore a shiny black suit and liked to carry a long cane. Williams then left for the Belfast Academy, before attending a private school in Greenwich. Information on his personal life is frustratingly scant but one thing for certain is that today's war correspondents owe a great deal to this 'soldier of the pencil'.

He began his career in journalism with the *Belfast News Letter*, which is today the oldest newspaper in the English-speaking world. (It was founded in Ballymena in 1737 by Francis Joy, a paper manufacturer and grandfather of the rebel, Henry Joy McCracken.) After cutting his teeth on the local news scene, Charles left for London; however, due to health concerns, it seems that he continued on to the southern states of America, where he took part in a 'filibustering' (unlawful military action) campaign led by the adventurer, William Walker (1824-1860).

Walker, a journalist and editor, who had fought three duels, decided to personally 'take' or conquer as much as he could of Latin America, where he would then create and rule over 'white' states. In fact, he became President of Nicaragua from 1856 to 1857.

The Phoenix Fountain.

The sun sets over Dunluce Castle.

Dunluce Castle by day.

Downhill.

Downhill.

Mount Sandel Forest.

Mount Sandel Fort.

Bertie Peacock in the Diamond, Coleraine.

The Joey Dunlop Memorial Garden, Ballymoney.

The Joey Dunlop Memorial Garden, Ballymoney.

Unfortunately, but possibly inevitably, he met a bad end in 1860 when he was executed by the Honduras government. Williams threw himself into the fighting in the initial campaign, earning a reputation as a daring blockade-runner. He returned to London where he was appointed 'leader-writer' with the *London Evening Herald*.

In October 1859 he began working with the *Standard*, which was soon to be re-christened *The Evening Standard*, a newspaper which banked its reputation on its exemplary reporting of foreign news, particularly its detailed commentaries on the likes of the American Civil War (1861-1865), the Prussian-Austrian War (1866) and the Franco-Prussian War (1870). Charles was mostly responsible for the first-hand coverage, and it was first-hand because he believed in reporting from the front line. This cannot have been easy on his wife, Georgina Goold Ward, whom he married in 1861. Georgina's mother, Anne Ward, had opened a stationery and book shop at the Diamond in 1852, and had also published the *Coleraine Almanac and Directory for 1861* and written a book entitled *Waves on the Ocean of Life*. Anne drowned in California in 1873, where she had retired as a widow. Her death was reported in the *San Francisco Weekly Bulletin* on 28 February:

> Tweed's stage while on its way to Julian on Monday last got mired in the evening, two miles this side of the crossing of Coleman's Creek. It contained three passengers, two ladies named Mrs Ward and Mrs Milne and a young man named Crowell. A terrific storm was raging at the time, rain and sleet were coming down in torrents. Mrs Ward and Mrs Milne attempted to cross the creek, but were swept away by the flood and drowned.

Georgina's retail background was something she had in common with her husband. His father ran a hardware store in the Diamond, while his grandmother, Mrs McKinley, had previously managed a delph shop in the same vicinity. This woman only died in 1867, at the fantastic age of 107!

In 1870, Charles was with the French Army of the Loire for what was the beginning of the second phase of the Franco-Prussian War, and he was one of only two correspondents in Strasbourg when it fell.

Seven years later, Williams spent time with the staff of Ahmed Mukhtar Pasha, the commander of the Turkish forces in Armenia. His series of letters back to the newspaper were the only source of information available to England, describing Mukhtar Pasha's subsequent defence of Constantinople against the Russians. The letters, which are notably pro-Turkish, were published in book form, *The Armenian Campaign*, in 1878. The Russo-Turkish war ended with the signing of the Treaty of San Stefano on 3 March 1878, in a small village west of Istanbul, and Williams was there to witness it. By this stage Williams was on first name terms with the Russian general, Mikhail Dmitrievich Skobelev (1843-1882), who became famous both for his conquest of Central Asia and his heroism during the war with the Turks. Apparently, Skobelev was always to be found in the very heart of the fiercest fighting—and he was easily seen, thanks to his habit of dressing from head to toe in white, while sitting astride his white horse, earning himself the nickname 'The White General' from his devoted soldiers. Today he is regarded by many to have been the best commander in the world from the period 1870 to 1914.

Meanwhile Williams had other places to go and people to see. By the end of 1878 he was in Afghanistan, the experiences of which resulted in his 1879 book, *Notes on the Operations in Lower Afghanistan 1878-9 With Special Reference to Transport*. A few years later, in 1884, he accompanied Lord Garnet Joseph Wolseley (1833-1913) across the Sudan in the desperate race against time to rescue the much-loved British general Charles 'Chinese' Gordon (1833-1855) who had been sent to city of Khartoum to commence evacuation of all foreigners. In 1881 the Egyptian province of Sudan rebelled against its Egyptian and British leaders and, as the situation grew increasingly more troublesome, the British prepared to let it go. When General Gordon arrived in Khartoum he immediately encountered a perilous situation; things were far, far worse than expected, so he called for military support. The British government, wavering over the cost of such an expedition, were obliged to give in to public demand and send help in the person of Lord Wolseley, the brilliant Field Marshal, whose name's synonymity with perfection inspired the nineteenth-century slogan, 'Everything's all Sir Garnet.'

Major-General Charles George Gordon was known by various names, thanks to his infamous campaigns in China and northern Africa: 'Chinese Gordon', 'Gordon Pasha', and 'Gordon of Khartoum'. He was a Christian evangelist who, when home, made a point of visiting the sick and elderly. He even set up a boy's club in Gravesend in Kent. A lifelong bachelor, he was small in stature, at five feet and five inches, with quirky religious theories which included a belief that God literally sat on a throne over the altar of the Temple in Jerusalem, while the Devil sat in an exactly corresponding location, near Pitcairn Island in the Pacific Ocean. The Garden of Eden, he fervently believed, was to be found on the island of Praslin in the Seychelles. (Hollywood actor Charlton Heston played Gordon in the 1966 film *Khartoum*.)

It was never going to be an easy task. Lord Wolseley had approximately seven thousand men, which he decided to divide into two groups: a river column and a desert column. The river column required a contingent of small wooden boats to be piloted by men specifically brought over from Canada, while the desert column was divided further, with the best men taken from fourteen regiments to travel on camels, a sort of 'flying column'—the first specialist force to be devised in British military history. There were immediate problems with this force since—naturally enough—not one British soldier was experienced in riding or handling bad-tempered, fiercely stubborn camels. Nevertheless, it was the desert column that did all the fighting, with two major battles at Abu Klea (then Abu Kru). The enemy had greater numbers in their ranks, but the British, led by the vastly inexperienced Colonel Sir Charles Wilson, managed to hold them off, fighting in square formations, until they finally reached the banks of the Nile. There, waiting for them, were two steamboats that had been sent by General Gordon. Colonel Wilson took just twenty men with him and they sailed to Khartoum, reaching the city on 29 January 1885. However, they were much too late; the city was in ruins and General Gordon had been beheaded two days earlier.

Charles Williams wrote about what happened for the periodical, *Fortnightly Review*, in May 1885. His article, 'How We Lost Gordon', blamed the unfortunate Sir Charles Wilson, along with an overall lack of British nerve.

The Coleraine man had left the *Evening Standard* in 1884, having edited it for his last three years there, and he had a brief engagement with the *Morning Advertiser*, before becoming war correspondent for *The Daily Chronicle*, a relatively new paper that had been founded in 1872. (One of its future reporters would be Sir Arthur Conan Doyle, the creator of Sherlock Holmes.) Typically, Williams was the only English correspondent to witness and report on the rather short war between Bulgaria and Serbia, which began on 14 November 1885, and finished fourteen days later, culminating in the Unification of Bulgaria on 6 September 1885. He seemed to have a peculiar knack for being in the right place at the right time.

Williams published his only novel, *John Thaddeus Mackay*, in

1889, and it would appear that he was thinking of his earlier days in Coleraine whilst writing it. The story concerns a northern Irish Presbyterian minister, a Protestant minister, and a Catholic priest who undertake a journey to India where they learn the true definition of charity.

Eight years later he was present for another war, the Greco-Turkish War of 1897, which is more widely known as the 'Thirty Days War'. Williams was with the Greek army in Thessaly where sixty thousand Turks were based, facing just forty-six thousand Greeks. In another article for *Fortnightly Review* in June 1897, he blamed politics for the subsequent Greek defeat. The European powers arranged for an end to the conflict between Greece and the Ottoman Empire with the signing of a peace treaty on 20 September.

Charles Williams was soon back in the city of Khartoum to report on Kitchener's Sudanese Campaign in 1898. The British government had given General Horatio Herbert Kitchener (1850-1916) their blessing to retrieve Sudan from the Mahdists. Williams sent back dramatic accounts to the *Chronicle* of the Battle of Omdurman, which lasted five hours and resulted in the loss of eleven thousand Mahdists and just forty-eight Anglo-Egyptians, and the British recapture of Khartoum in 1898.

By this stage Williams was not just a famous war correspondent; he was also revered as a military expert. His health prevented him from one last hoorah, covering the Boer War in South Africa. Nevertheless, he followed events closely, writing up his comments in diary form for the *Morning Leader*. Later, in 1902, he published a pamphlet, *Hushed Up*, which condemned the level of secrecy that surrounded this conflict. Williams was clearly not afraid to make enemies. A religious man, he had presented Bishop Creighton (1843-1901), the bishop of London and an English historian of renown, with an ivory and gold mitre that he had himself designed, as thanks for his safe return from Khartoum. He was much sought after by newspapers and periodicals for his military articles, and even embarked on a public-speaking tour in America, where he thrilled audiences with stories of the wars and campaigns he had reported on. He was described by one eyewitness as having a 'bronzed' and 'grizzled' appearance, looking more like a soldier or sailor than a writer. Almost as a matter of course he dabbled in politics, going up against a Mr Herbert Gladstone (the future prime minister) for a position in West Leeds, but it was not to be. In 1893 he was appointed as Chairman of the Institute of Journalists, a position he held for just one year. Then, in 1896, he founded, and was President of, the London Press Club. One account describes him as possessing an 'irascible temper', which might not be surprising after the life he had lived.

Charles Williams died in his Brixton lodgings on 9 February 1904. His passing was noted in newspapers across the western world, including *The New York Times*, which printed a brief summary of the Coleraine man's career. His two sons were definitely a chip off the old block in that they both travelled far and wide, and found employment in the newspaper business. One son worked for a Sydney paper while the other, Frederick Henry, lived in Montreal, married a Canadian girl in 1886, and worked for the local newspaper.

Mary Alice Young (1867-1946)

was born Mary Alice McNaghten and grew up on the spacious eight thousand-acre family estate at Dundarave, in Bushmills. Her father was Sir Francis Edward Workman McNaghten (for whom the McNaghten Baronetcy was created on 16 July 1836), and a future descendent of his would inadvertently propel a young Private Robert Quigg to risk his life several times on a French battlefield in 1916 (*see* **Origins**).

Today Dundarave country house is still home to the McNaghten family and is believed to be the largest house in Northern Ireland that remains a private residence. It was built in 1846 to the design of renowned Victorian architect, Sir Charles Lanyon (1813-1889). There are four gate-lodges, two of which probably belonged to the extant Bushmills House, while the other two, which are bigger and more fanciful, were designed by Sir Charles.

Lanyon was born in Eastbourne in Sussex, and then moved to Dublin in the 1830s to take up a position as a civil engineer with the Irish Board of Works. He spent some time in County Kildare as the County Surveyor before moving to Antrim to perform the same duties. Some of his projects from this time include the coast road between Larne and Portrush, the Belfast to Ballymena railway line, the Belfast to Bangor line, and the Belfast Queen's and Ormeau bridges. This was only the beginning. He was a man of vision and obviously loved his work. In the 1840s he set up his own architectural firm and began to design and erect a long list of buildings in Belfast that are still standing proud today: the Linen Hall Library, Belfast Castle, Queen's College (the Lanyon Buildings of Queen's University), the Crumlin Road Courthouse and Gaol, the Palm House in the Botanic Gardens, Stranmillis House, and the Public Library in Royal Avenue, to name but a few. Never one to stay too long in a job, he exchanged his architect's career for politics and became Lord Mayor of Belfast in 1862. Six years later he was knighted. He died in his house in Whiteabbey in 1889 and was buried at Newtownbreda Churchyard.

Mary Alice clearly belonged to the gentry and was, therefore, bound to socialise only with those from her own class. As such she married into another wealthy family in 1893, the Youngs of Ballymena. Her father-in-law, the Right Honourable John Young, who was a Privy Councillor, Deputy Lieutenant and Justice of the Peace, owned Galgorm Castle with the surrounding estate of two thousand acres, and it was his eldest son, W R, who became Mary's husband. Three years later they had a daughter, Hilda Grace. Previously, her in-laws had been hugely successful merchants in Ballymena and had only bought the castle in 1850 from the Earl of Mountcashel, but they were an established landed family of the upper classes by the time that Mary Alice was introduced to them. When her father-in-law died in 1915 his eldest son took over the castle and estate, allowing Mary to incorporate her grand new home into her favourite hobby. Young women from moneyed backgrounds usually spent their free time in the genteel occupations of embroidery or dabbling with watercolours. Mary, however, was a disciple of the relatively modern art of photography.

She took over a thousand photographs between 1890 and 1915, most of which had her family, friends and the day-to-day life on the Galgorm estate as their subject, and included portraits of the gardeners, gamekeepers, coachmen, labourers and servants. Her work documents the grand life that was enjoyed by the gentry in those blissful years before the horror of World War One, and there are lots of photographs of her relatives and friends playing tennis or croquet, or fishing. One photo shows her sister Hilda, in 1900, sitting in a cornfield, busily working at her watercolours, while a later photograph, from 1907, shows her daughter sewing in her nursery. The sewing basket that she is making good use of was actually her Christmas present from the family grocer in Galgorm.

Mary's photography is noted particularly for its experimentation with 'chiaroscuro', which is basically the deliberate use of shadow and light. 'Chiaroscuro' is derived from the Italian words for 'bright or clear' and 'dark or obscure'. The technique was first used by Renaissance painters, who strove to paint the illusion of three dimensions using a variety of tones and careful shading. For instance, an ordinary artist might paint a black car on a sunny day as being just black, whereas the talented painter would know that it would be more truthful to paint a black car with white spots where the sunlight bounces off it; also, there will probably be the merest hint of blue, thanks to the reflection of a cloudless sky, not to mention the other colours from the car's surroundings.

Being the lady of the manor, however, was not a part-time job. Mary was kept busy with taking care of her family, managing the domestic and grounds' staff, and taking care of her husband's relatives. His five brothers and seven sisters regularly descended upon Galgorm Castle for long visits, which meant more work for its overall supervisor. It seems that she turned from photography forever with the advent of the Second World War. Despite her age—she was seventy-two in 1939—she threw herself into war work, giving up all her free time to organise benefits for the troops. Then, in 1946, just a year after the war had ended, she passed away. Her legacy prevails today in the form of her invaluable collection of photographs.

PART THREE

AROUND COLERAINE

For the wandering tourist and the curious resident, there are many places of interest just outside the town of Coleraine, and here are just a few of them.

Dunluce Castle

This has been described as being probably the most picturesque castle on the island. There is certainly something thoroughly majestic about the roofless ruins that sit on the utmost edge of a rock peninsula that juts out from the North Antrim coast. Originally the castle consisted of a rectangular courtyard with sturdy walls, towers, and several buildings. Its precarious location added to its overall impression as an impenetrable fortress. Even if intruders managed to get through to the interior, the getaway boat was waiting, out of sight, in the sea cave below.

The cliff on which the castle is built is thirty metres high, and is made of much softer stuff that the hardy basalt of the Giant's Causeway. Therefore, erosion is a common occurrence—which is information that Duchess Catherine Manners could, in retrospect, have done with. In 1620 Sir Randall MacDonnell was appointed as Earl of Antrim. He was a favourite with James VI of Scotland, who was to become King James I of England. One of MacDonnell's duties as Earl was to build a castle in each of his baronies, and he decided to take the opportunity to carry out a complete renovation at Dunluce, his family's castle, including the construction of the new manor house. This Manor House had a Great Hall with two fireplaces, three bow windows, and a large timber staircase that led to the upper private quarters. Fifteen years later, in 1635, Sir Randall's son married the Duke of Buckingham's widow, Catherine Manners, and brought her to live in the castle. The Duchess was used to the finer things in life and was not too thrilled to find herself perched on a rocky peninsula, listening to the roar of the sea below. She hated the sea, it made her nervous; furthermore, what she hated even more than the sea itself was the sound that it made as it lapped against the ragged rocks of the Causeway Coast.

Nevertheless, Catherine was an obedient wife and wanted to please her new husband. We don't know how she felt following a few years of living at Dunluce, whether she had become used to her new home, or whether it still unnerved her, but it ultimately doesn't matter, as we can pretty much gauge her feelings after a party that she and her husband threw in 1639.

The story goes that it was a big important dinner which required lots of preparation and supervision of staff. It was also a stormy night and maybe Catherine experienced some queasiness as she heard the waves crashing into the rocks far beneath her feet. In the midst of all the celebrations she had to go into the kitchen to give some orders to the cooks. The kitchen was in the most northerly part of the castle and, presumably, its exterior was more prone to the battering of the wind and the rain. There are slightly differing versions of what happened next, but perhaps the most popular one is that, just as Catherine was speaking to the cook, the edge of the kitchen gave way, falling down into the sea, taking various members of her staff with it, including the very cook whom Catherine had been conversing with. This was a horrifying experience for all who witnessed it, not least, of course, for Catherine herself!

Naturally enough, there are those who claim that the ruins are haunted today by the screams of the servants and cooks who were flung to their deaths on that dreadful night.

The Giant's Causeway

By far the most popular tourist spot in the North of Ireland, the Causeway was voted the fourth greatest natural wonder in the United Kingdom by readers of the *Radio Times* magazine in 2005, while it came top of the poll for the 2007 UTV programme, *Ultimate Ulster: Ten Best Places*, as voted for by viewers, beating the likes of the Mourne Mountains and Strangford Lough. It is the only UNESCO World Heritage Site to be found in Northern Ireland.

The Causeway is over sixty millions years old but was only discovered in 1692 by an early Bishop of Derry, who immediately brought it to the attention of interested parties in Dublin and London. A year later it received instant fame after Sir Richard Bukeley, a fellow at Trinity College, presented a paper to the Royal Society about this fantastic discovery and generated a debate about how the Causeway was formed.

The Dublin Society was founded by members of the Dublin Philosophical Society, and its principal aim was the promotion of the arts, agriculture, industry, and science in Ireland. It became the Royal Dublin Society in 1820 when George IV became Society Patron. Fifty-nine years later the Society acquired the premises at Ballsbridge, Dublin 4, where it still currently resides, although the area it inhabits has expanded somewhat from the original fifteen acres to today's forty.

Dublin artist Susanna Drury (1698–1770) contributed to the Causeway's growing international fame when she painted it in 1740. She travelled north and spent several months studying the forty thousand or so basalt columns that form a sort of massive, intricate stony staircase, which continues all the way down into the depths of the Atlantic Ocean. The Dublin Society made her the recipient of their first award, with the result that her paintings were subsequently seen by a wider audience, and reproduced in 1743 and 1744 when engravings were made of them. (The Ulster Museum recently acquired two of her drawings.) In 1765 her Causeway landscape was used for the French *Encyclopédie*, where it was included in the geology section with a comment by the French expert Nicolas Desmarest (1725–1815) who proposed, for the first time in print, that the site had been created as a result of a volcanic eruption.

Of course, other commentators point to a more credible explanation for the Causeway's existence, insisting that it was built by the Irish giant, Finn McCool, who needed to get to across the water to fight the Scottish giant, Benandonner. Being a practical man with initiative, he built himself a causeway of stepping stones. Naturally he was very tired after all the building and needed to sleep before he could finish his quest. Unfortunately, Benandonner, the bigger of the two behemoths, grew impatient and came over to confront him. Finn's wife, Oonagh, a resourceful woman if ever there was one, saw him approaching and threw a—presumably large—blanket over her sleeping husband, pretending to the Scot that he was her infant son. When Benandonner saw the size of the 'baby', he immediately assumed that its father must be ridiculously huge. He turned right around and ran back to Scotland at great speed, tearing up the causeway in terror as he went.

Tourism in the area really took off when the Giant's Causeway Tramway was launched in 1887, which linked the site to Portrush and Bushmills. It is said that the early visitors used to complain about the difficulty in reaching the isolated spot. However, when it was discovered that one could stop in Bushmills to wisely fortify oneself with the local 'water of life' against the harsh natural elements associated with the trek, they were a lot more amenable to the journey, and perhaps even looked forward to it. Before its closure in 1949, the tramline had been the longest running electric track of its type in existence.

Downhill and Mussenden Temple

There is something intriguing about Frederick Hervey. The more one learns about him, the more one wants to keep digging for information on this man. Born in 1730 (d.1803) he was made Bishop of Derry when he was thirty-eight years of age. Ten years later, in 1778, after the death of his brother Augustus (who was also the Lord Lieutenant of Ireland), the Bishop inherited an Earldom (of Bristol), making him the first 'Earl Bishop' for seven centuries, and a wealthy one at that.

A man of many interests, the Bishop was a keen amateur geologist. He was also passionate about art, and travelled extensively, building up a lavish collection of books and paintings. Architecture was another interest, particularly of the religious kind. With the help of his wages from the diocese he tended to the churches in his care, and most of them had a spire at the time of his death. He was nicknamed the 'Edifying Bishop' on account of all the construction work he commissioned, including the 'Bishop's Road', which stretches from Downhill across Benevenagh Mountain towards Limavady. And then there were the more elaborate projects.

Hervey began work on a house at Downhill at some point in the 1770s; certain accounts claim 1775 as the start date, while others state it was the year 1778 in which the foundation stone of the house with 'as many windows as there are days in the year' was laid. All in all, £80,000 was spent. There was a huge library to house the Bishop's books, while the walls of the house were covered in painted frescoes or with examples from Hervey's impressive collection of paintings by the likes of Van Dyke, Rubens, Raphael and Tintoretto. He left Ireland in 1791 with the aim of collecting great paintings for his houses, and somehow managed to get himself arrested by Napoleon, who thought he was a spy. He reclaimed his freedom, but at a price; £18,000 worth of paintings were confiscated from him. Not everyone agreed with his choice of bleak location, or even with the house itself. At least one visitor found it a forbidding construction, writing that he had 'never seen so bad a house occupy as much ground'.

When the house was completed the Bishop started working on a new building, the Mussenden Temple, which sits on top of the cliff. It was to be a sort of ornamental summer library built in honour of his fair cousin, Mrs Frideswide Mussenden. The temple is an exact copy of the Italian Temple of Vesta; Vesta is the Roman goddess of the hearth, and thus, the home. The original stands in the forum in Rome, and its design was a replica of the first Roman houses, which were round huts made from mud and straw. There is an inscription around the dome of the Hervey temple by the Roman poet Lucretius (approximately 94–55BC), and translated by the English poet John Dryden (1631–1700):

'Tis pleasant, safely to behold from shore
The rolling ship, and hear the tempest roar.

However, it is not so safe now, or so far from the 'tempest roar'. The National Trust, in whose care Mussenden is today, had to have extensive work completed on the cliffs to strengthen them, and to prevent the temple from disappearing down into the sea below, such was the danger of erosion. It used to be possible to drive all the way around the temple in a horse and cart, but that was a hundred years ago, and definitely would not be encouraged now—unless you really disliked the horse.

Naturally, this project raised more than a few eyebrows since

Bishop Hervey and Mrs Mussenden were both married to other people; despite the rumours, it is generally believed that their relationship was platonic. In any case, Mrs Mussenden didn't live long enough to see the finished article, dying as she did, aged only twenty-two.

There was undoubtedly further scandal when it was discovered that the Church of Ireland Bishop had a room installed beneath the library which was specifically for the use of Catholic priests to say Mass. He believed in supporting all religions, and even advocated Catholic Emancipation. During the political and religious turbulence of the late 1770s and early 1780s, the Bishop involved himself temporarily, taking the side of the Irish Volunteers, shocking even them with his rousing speeches. By 1780 his wife had left him, possibly as a result of his support for underdog causes and passionate empathy with the 'wrong side' on certain issues. He was considered a genuine eccentric, showing his love for, and tolerance of, all religious denominations by organising a horse-race between the local priests and reverends. Now, that would have been a sight to behold!

Portstewart

Located three miles from Coleraine, this attractive and busy little seaside town started out as a quiet fishing village in the possession of John Cromie, a local wine merchant, who decided in the early nineteenth century to develop its attractions as a 'watering place'. Stephen Cromie, John's father, had originally bought the land from the Stewart family in Ballyleese. This is how the town got its name.

In 1734, Lieutenant Stewart obtained a lease of the area from the Earl of Antrim. Accordingly, John had 'good houses' built for the summer visitors. Then, as you can imagine, once the railway arrived in 1855 there was a considerable boost in business and tourism. Since none of the locals wished to play host to the railway tracks on their land it was necessary to build the station a mile away with a steam tram that carried passengers straight to the promenade.

Apart from being a popular holiday destination, Portstewart was also a busy fishing port right up to the Second World War. Meanwhile, the famous two-mile stretch of Portstewart Strand was once home to Neolithic and Iron Age people, excavations beneath the sand-hills producing evidence in the form of flints, arrowheads, and shards of pottery. Items such as bronze pins and Roman jewellery, which were also found here, point to a later generation of dwellers. Nowadays, the Strand is an important conservation site, rich in plants and insects.

At the end of the Strand is Tubber Patrick, St Patrick's Well, which was probably the source of fresh water for the Strand's ancient dwellers. It also provided a source of income for thrifty locals, who would sell water to thirsty tourists in the 1940s.

Portstewart is heavily identified with the very serious game of golf. There are three golf courses under the banner of the famous Portstewart Golf Club, where golfers battle with each other and the frequently more troublesome Atlantic winds. The club also boasts one of Europe's few fifty-four hole courses. A particular favourite is the Strands course, with its breathtaking views that stretch as far as the Inishowen peninsula in Donegal. The Club is extremely proud of this course, and so it should be. It is ranked number ninety-five on the list of the top one hundred courses in the British Isles. Some say that it provides the best opening hole in Ireland, while others go further and say it's the best opening hole in the world.

USEFUL WEBSITES

www.aghamoreireland.com
www.carothersonline.com
www.colerainefc.com
www.fathom.com
www.geocites.com
www.gorrygallery.ie
www.henrymccullough.com
www.irelandseye.com
www.maddbenn.com
www.nationalarchives.co.uk
www.potstill.de
www.query.nytimes.com
www.rascal.ac.uk
www.thegordonhighlanders.co.uk
www.vlib.us
www.whistler.arts.gla.ac.uk
www.wineandwhisky.co.uk

BIBLIOGRAPHY

Ashcroft, Michael; *Victoria Cross Heroes*: Headline Review, London, 2006

Bardon, Jonathan; *A History of Ulster*: Blackstaff Press, Belfast, 2005

Citizens' Committee; *The Great War: A Tribute to Ulster's Heroes 1914-1918*: Pretani Press, Belfast, 1991

Coleraine Historical Society; *Ordnance Survey Memoir for the parish of Coleraine*: Coleraine, 1986

Coleraine Town Partnership; *Round The Ramparts: A Walking Heritage Guide*: Cranagh Press, 2002

Hayes, Dean; *Northern Ireland's Greats: 100 Top Football Heroes*: Appletree Press, Belfast, 2005

Lee, Sydney; *Dictionary of National Biography, Vol III*: Elibron Classics

McCook, Alistair; *The Power And The Glory: The History of the North West 200*: Appletree Press, Belfast, 2002

McKay, Patrick; *A Dictionary of Ulster Place Names*: Cló Ollscoil na Banríona, Queen's University, Belfast, 2007

Moore, Steven; *The Irish on the Somme*: Local Press, Belfast, 2005

Mullin, T H; *Coleraine in Georgian Times*: Belfast, 1979

Mullin, T H; *Coleraine in Modern Times*: Belfast, 1977

Newman, Kate: *Dictionary of Ulster Biography*: Institute of Irish

Studies, Queen's University, Belfast, 1993

Orr, David R; *Duty Without Glory: Ulster's Home Guard in the Second World War and the Cold War*: Redcoat, 2008

Pierce, Nicola; *Ballymena: City of The Seven Towers*: Brehon Press, Belfast, 2007

Townsend, Brian; *The Lost Distilleries of Ireland*: Neil Wilson Publishing, Glasgow, 1999

Wallace, Martin, *Famous Irish Writers*; Appletree Press, Belfast, 1999

Index

Abbey Street *17, 28*

Abraham, James Johnston *45, 46, 47*
   Surgeon's Journey 45

Adams, Ellen *47*

Adams, John Bodkins *47, 48, 49,*
   50, 51, 52, 53, 54

Adams, Samuel *47, 48*

Adams, William *48*

Afghan War *21*

(80th) Airborne Anti-Aircraft
Artillery Battalion *25*

Alexander, Rev Nat *33*

Allingham, William *54, 55, 56*
   Day and Night Songs 55
   Fifty Modern Poems 56
   'Laurence Bloomfield in Ireland' *55*
   Poems 55
   'The Fairies' *56*
   'The Music Master' *55*

American Revolutionary War *83,*
   88, 97

Amiens *23*

Ancre British Cemetery *23*

Andrews, Catherine *94*

Animals, the *64*

Ashbrook *23*

Astor Place Opera House *69, 70*

Austen, Jane *95*
   Emma 96
   Pride and Prejudice 95

Ballymena Guardian, the *29*

Ballymena United *79*

Bann, River *13, 16*

Bannen, Ian *77*

Baron of Dungannon
   see O'Neill, Hugh

Barret Browing, Elizabeth *56*

Barret Browning, Robert *56*

Barrett, Laurence *72*

Barrie, J M *95*

Bateman, Colin *78*

Battle of Chrasia *21*

Battle of Kandahar *22*

Battle of Omdurman *101*

Battle of the Somme *22*

Beatles, the *64*

Beatty, Ned *76*

Belfast News Letter 34, *96*

Bell, Fanny Jane *23*

Bell, James *23*

Bell, Second Lieutenant William
James Knox *23*

Benandonner *112*

Bent, Geoff *62*

Beresford, Tristram *16*

Bertrancourt Military Cemetery *23*

Best, George *62, 80*

Billy Parish Churchyard *25*

Bingham, Billy *80*

Black, Thomas *36*

(6th) Black Watch *23*

Blanchflower, Jackie *62*

Boer War *21*

Bonaparte, Napoleon *114*

Bond, Frederic *74, 75*

Booth, Edwin Thomas *71*

Booth, John Wilkes *71*

Boothenian Dramatic Association *68*

Boswell, James *56*

Boyd, Anna Arabella *57*

Boyd, Dr John *35, 56, 57, 58, 59*

Boyd Street
   see Newmarket Street

Boyd, William *37*

Bridge Street *17, 54*

British Empire Medal (BEM) *26*
Bristol Royal Infirmary *48*
Brooke Street *36*
Bukeley, Richard *111*
Burdon, Eric *66*
Burns, Darren *39*
'Busby's Babes' *60, 61*
Busby, Matt *60, 62*
Bushmills *23, 112*
Bushmills Distillery *34, 37*
Byrne, Roger *62*

Camp Cromore *25*
Campbell Brothers *19*
Cannon, Barney *79*
Carlyle, Thomas *55, 56*
Carnkirk *23*
Carothers, Arthur *90*
Caterpillar Valley Cemetery *25*
Celtic Football Club *79, 80*
Chandler, Chas *64*
Charlton, Bobby *61, 62*
Charter of the Irish Society *17*
Chichester, Sir Arthur *14*
Christ, Jesus *27*
Christie, Daniel Hall *33*
Church Street *17, 23, 29*
Circular Road Junction *54*
City of Derry and District Motor
    Club *39*
City Hall, Belfast's *19*
Clark, George Rogers *84, 87*
Clarke, Andrew *37*
Clay, Harry *27*
Cocker, Joe *65*
Coleraine Almanac, the *31, 97*
'Coleraine Battery' *26*
Coleraine Borough Council *96*
Coleraine Chronicle, the *27, 28, 58, 59*
Coleraine Constitution, the
    see *Northern Constitution*, the

Coleraine Council *33*
Coleraine Football Club *59, 79*
Coleraine Museum *96*
Collier, Thomas Frederick *92*
Colman, Eddie *62*
Controller of Customs *54*
Cooke, Dr R O *46*
Cork Examiner 92, *93*
Cromie, John *115*
Cromie, Stephen *115*
Crewe Alexandra *63*
Cross Lane *96*
Crimean War *21*
Coleraine Whiskey *36, 37*
'Cranford School' *95*
Creighton, Bishop *101*
Cromore Road *29*
Cumberland County *81, 87*
Customs House *54, 55*

Dallas, Private Edward Reid *23*
Dallas, Robert *31*
Dance, George (the Elder) *17*
Deady, Winifred *88*
Delavillebeuvre, Juan *87*
Derry Journal, the *28*
Desmarest, Nicolas *112*
Diamond, the *13, 19, 23, 29, 36, 97*
Dickens, Charles *56, 95*
Dirty Lane *35*
Doherty, Peter *80*
Doncaster Rovers *59*
Donovan *65*
Downhill *113*
Doyle, Sir Arthur Conan *100*
Dunbar, Adrian *76*
Dundarave Estate *23, 102, 103*
Dundooan House *57, 59*
Dunlop, David *29, 30*
Dunlop, Joey *38, 39, 40*
Dunlop, Robert *38, 39, 40*

Dunlop, (Captain) William *29*
Dunluce Castle *109*, *110*
Drury, Susanna *111*
Drydon, John *114*

Earl of Tyrone
   see O'Neill, Hugh
Ebenezer House *48*
Edwards, Duncan *62*
Eire Apparent *64*
Eliot, George *95*

Faithfull, Marianne *66*
Ferrar, Michael *36*
Festival Rose d'Or *77*
First World War *21*, *60*, *104*
Fitzgerald, Tara *76*
Fleadh Cowboys, the *66*
Flight of the Earls *14*
Forrest, Edwin *68*, *69*, *71*, *72*
Fort Bute *86*
Fort Manchac *86*
Foulkes, Bill *62*
Franco-Prussian War (1870) *97*, *98*
Franklin, Benjamin *84*
Fraser's Magazine 56
Frode, J A *56*

Gage, William *16*
Galgorm Castle *103*
Galgorm Estate *104*
Gálvez, de Don Bernardo *85*, *86*, *87*
Gaskell, Elizabeth *95*
   Cranford 95
Giant's Causeway *23*, *109*, *111*, *112*
Gilmour, Second Lieutenant Robert
Wallace *22*
Given, Robert *31*
Gladstone, Herbert *102*
Glentoran Football Club *79*
Golden Rose of Montreux *77*

Goldsmith, Oliver *95*
   The Vicar of Wakefield 95
Gordon, Charles 'Chinese' *99*
Gordon Highlanders, 92nd
Regiment of *21*
Gordon Highlanders Museum *22*
Great Irish Famine *26*, *69*, *93*
Great Universal Stores (GUS) *37*
Greco-Turkish War (1897) *101*
Gregg, Harry *59*, *60*, *61*, *62*, *63*
   Harry's Game 63
Griffith, Maria *33*
Guildhall, Derry's *19*

Hamel *23*, *24*
Hannynton, T K *32*
Haworth, Joseph *73*
Hawthorne, Nathaniel *95*
Hendrix, Jimi *64*
Henry, Florence *48*
Henry, Patrick *84*
Henson, Leslie *50*
Hervey, Augustus *113*
Hervey, Frederick *113*, *114*, *115*
Heston, Charlton *99*
   Khartoum 99
Hezlett, Rev Robert *57*
Higginson, Reverend *96*
Holmes, Sherlock *100*
Honourable Irish Society *13*, *14*,
   17, *19*
Hopkins, Gerard Manley *26*
House of Commons *36*
Hullet, Alfred John *50*
Hullett, Gertrude *50*, *51*, *52*
Hunt, Leigh *55*

Ice Age *20*
Innes, Janet *32*
Iron Age *116*

Jackson Hall *31, 32*
Jackson, George *32*
Jackson, Richard *32*
Jackson, William *32*
Jennings, Pat *80, 81*
Jones, Mark *62*
Joy, Francis *96*

Kelly, David *77*
Killowen *34*
Killowen Distillery *37*
Kilrea *25, 34*
King George IV *91, 111*
King James I *14, 15, 17, 109*
King James VI
   see King James I
Kirwian, Dervla *77*
Kitchener, General Horatio Herbert
   101
Knox, Charles *33*

Laine, Denny *65*
Lane, Denny *93*
Landsdowne Crescent *25*
Lane, Ronnie *66*
Lanyon, Sir Charles *103*
Lee, Charles *85*
Lee, Chauncey *89*
Leicester City *60, 62*
Lennox, Maria *94*
London Evening Herald 97
Leonard, Victor *81*
(6th) Light Anti-Aircraft Battery
Supplementary Reserve *26*
Lincoln, Abraham *71*
Litton, Edward *57*
Locke, Josef *76*
London Press Club *102*
*Londonderry Sentinel and North West
Advertiser*, the *28*
London-Derry Journal and General

Advertiser, the *27, 28*
Lord Burghley 60
Lower Stone Road *28*
Lowney, Declan *76*
Lukic, Venona *61, 63*
Lukic, Vera *61, 63*
Lukic, Zoran *63*

Macari, Lou *63*
MacDonnell, Sir Randall *109*
Mackay, Hugh Boyd *28*
Macready, William Charles *69, 70,
   71*
Mailly Wood Cemetery *23*
Manchester United *60, 63, 79*
Manor House
   see Jackson Hall
Manners, Duchess Catherine *109,
   110*
Mansion House *17*
Market House *17, 18, 19*
Marquis of Waterford *18*
Matthews, Joseph *31*
Maxwell, Mrs *31, 33*
Mawhood, William *48*
McBride, Susan *29*
McCartney, Lynda *65, 66*
McCartney, Paul *65, 66*
McCombie, John *28*
McCool, Finn *112*
McCracken, Henry Joy *96*
McCullough, Elizabeth *67*
McCullough, Henry *63, 64, 65, 66*
McCullough, James *67*
McCullough, Jane *67*
McCullough, John Edward *67, 68,
   72, 73, 74, 75*
McCullough, Mary *67*
McCullough, William *72*
McElfatrick, Mrs *31*
McLaughlin & Harvey *19*

McNaghten, (Second Lieutenant Sir) Arthur Douglas 25
McNaghten, (Second Lieutenant Sir) Edward Harry 23, 24, 25
McNaghten, Sir Francis Edward Workman 102
McNaghten, (Sir) Harry 23
McNaghten, Mary Alice
   see Mary Alice Young
McQuigg, Malcolm 40
Mecklenburg County 27
Mesolithic Period 20
Middle Earth Club 64
Miller, Frankie 66
Millais, John Everett 55
Miller, Thomas Knox 26
Miller, William 27
Mitchell, William 29
Mitford, Mary Russell 95
   Our Village 95
Model School 94
Monash, General 24
Moody Blues, the 65
Moore, James 36
Morning Leader, the 101
Morrell, Edith Alice 51, 52, 53
Morris, Robert 84, 85, 87, 88, 89
Morse, Samuel 26
Mount Sandel 20, 48
Mussenden, Frideswide 114, 115
Mussenden Temple 114

National Health Service 53
National Theatre 74
National Trust 114
Nesbitt, James 76, 77, 78, 79
New Row 17
Newmarket Street 35
Nietzsche, Frederick 26
No 2 Londonderry County Battalion 26

North West 200 38, 39
Northern Constitution, the 29, 31
Northern Standard, the 28
Northern Whig, the 28

O'Brien, Margaret 81
O'Cahans 13, 14, 15
Old Bailey 52
Old Comrades' Association 26
O'Neill clan 14, 15
O'Neill, Hugh 14, 17
O'Reilly, Governor-General Don Alejandro 81, 82
Ordnance Survey 29

(507th) Parachute Infantry Regiment Troopers 25
(508th) Parachute Infantry Regiment Troopers 25
Pasch, Gustaf Erik 27
Pasha, Ahmed Mukhtar 98
Paterson, Helen 56
Patrick, Saint 13, 116
Peacock, Robert 'Bertie' 79, 80, 81
Pegg, David 62
People, the 64
Phillips, Sir Thomas 15, 34
Pink Floyd 64, 66
   Dark Side of the Moon 66
Plantation of Coleraine 14
Polk, James K 27
Pollock, Oliver 81, 82, 83, 84, 85, 86, 87, 88, 89, 90
Polymesis Hospital 46
Portadown 64
Portrush 25, 38, 39, 112
Portstewart 21, 25, 38, 39, 63, 115
Portstewart Golf Club 116
Portstewart Strand 116
Poziers Memorial to the Missing 22, 23

Procol Harum *64*
Prussian-Austrian War (1866) *97*
Pynnar, Nicholas *17*

Queen Elizabeth *62*
Queen Victoria *26*
Queens University Belfast *48*
Quigg, Private Robert *23, 24, 25*
Quigg, Robert (Snr) *23, 102*

Rainbach, David Wilkie *91*
Red Cross *45, 47*
Red Star Belgrade *60*
Reid, Dr Thomas *31*
Rennie, John *35*
Rice, Tim *65*
Riem Airport *60*
Riverside Theatre *76*
Robinson, George V *28*
Robinson, John *30*
Rodgers, George *61*
Rolling Stones, the *64*
Rossetti, Dante Gabriel *55*
Rowley, John *16*
Royal Army Medical Corps
(RAMC) *45*
Royal Exchange *26*
Royal Hibernian Academy *91*
Royal Inniskilling Fusiliers *22*
Royal Irish Rifles, 12th Battalion *23*
Rutter, Michael *38*

Salomon, Haym *87, 88*
San Francisco Weekly Bulletin 97
Second World War *25, 26, 37, 105*
Seven Years War *83*
Seventh-Day Adventist Church *27*
Sexton, Dave *63*
Shakespeare *67, 95*
Shannon, Alfred *28*
Shannon, Bob *28*

Shannon, John *28*
Shannon, John (snr) *28*
Shannon, Tom *28*
Sharpe, Robert *31*
Sheil, Edward *91, 92, 93*
Sheil, George *92*
Sheridan, Richard Brinsley *95*
Shrewsbury Town *63*
(9th) Siege Battery Royal Garrison
Artillery *23*
Sillito, Rev William *31*
Simms, J H *29*
Singleton, Major Raymond *25*
Skobelev, Mikhail Dmitrievich *98*
Skyrockets, the *63*
Slade *65*
'Spanish Lady' *48*
'Spanish Milled Dollar' *89*
Spartacus *68, 72, 73*
Specht, Eddie *75*
Spooky Tooth *66*
Spring-Heeled Jack
    see Marquis of Waterford
St Botolph-without-Bishopsgate *17*
St Matthews' Church *17*
Stoke City *63*
Stone Age *20*
Swansea City *63*
Sweeney's Men *65*
Swindon Town *63*

Taylor, Robert *36, 37*
Taylor, Tommy *62*
Tennyson, Lord Alfred *55*
Thackeray, William *96*
    Vanity Fair 96
The Daily Chronicle 100
The English Illustrated Magazine 94
The Evening Standard 97, 100
The New York Times 102
The Sunday Times 64

'Thirty Days War'
    see Greco-Turkish War (1897)
Thistle, Patrick *80*
Thompson, Dr James *56*
Thomson, Hugh *94, 95*
Toome *15*
Topp, George *36*
Town Hall *19, 21, 31, 58*
Townsend, Brian
    The Lost Distilleries of Ireland 37
Treaty of San Stefano *98*
Treves, Sir Frederick *45*
Trinity College Dublin *45, 111*
Troy, Cyril *29*
Troy, James *28*
Troy, Robert J *29*
Troy, Samuel Selfridge *29*
Troy, Samuel Selfridge (jnr) *29*
Tubber Patrick *116*
Turgenev, Ivan *56*
Turner, Thomas *19*
Tyrone Constitution, the *27*

Ulster Bank *23*
Ulster Gazette, the *27*
Ulster Museum *112*
United Irishmen *32*
University of Ulster *29, 76, 79*
USAT *James Parker 25*

Victoria Cross *21, 22, 23, 25*
Vinycomb, John *94*
Viollett, Dennis *61*

Wallen, William *28*
Walker, William *96*
War Memorial *21*
Ward, Anne *31, 36, 97*
    Waves on the Ocean of Life 97
Ward, Francis *36*
Ward, Georgina *32, 97*

Ward, Marcus *31, 94*
Washington, George *84*
Washington Post, the *74*
Waterstone's *29*
Webber, Andrew Lloyd *65*
    Jesus Christ Superstar 65
Weir, Jim *81*
Whelan, Liam *62*
White, Marshall Sir George Stuart *21*
Whiteside, Rev John *31*
Whitton, Matilda *49*
Wilkie, Sir David *91*
Wilkinson, Private Arnold *23*
Williams, Charles *32, 96, 97, 98,*
100, 101, 102
    Hushed Up 101
    John Thaddeus Mackay 100
    Notes on the Operation
        in Lower Afghanistan 98
    The Armenian Campaign 98
Williams, Frederick Henry *102*
Wilson, Colonel Sir Charles *100*
Wilson, Ross *81*
Windson Park Swifts Football Club
    59
Windsor Hotel *63*
Wings *65*
    Red Rose Speedway 66
Wolfson, Isaac *37*
Wolseley, Lord Garnet Joseph *98, 99*
Woodstock *65*
World Cup, 1958 *62*

Yeats, William Butler *56*
Young, Hilda Grace *104*
Young, (Right Honourable) John *103*
Young, Mary Alice *102, 103, 104, 105*
Young, W R *104*